POWER
Politics

The electricity crisis and you

T0363971

POWER
Politics

The electricity crisis and you

edited by

JOHN SPOEHR

**Wakefield
Press**

Wakefield Press
Box 2266
Kent Town
South Australia 5071
www.wakefieldpress.com.au

First published 2003

Designed and typeset by Clinton Ellicott, Wakefield Press
Cover designed by Liz Nicholson, design BITE
Printed and bound by Hyde Park Press

National Library of Australia
Cataloguing-in-publication entry

Power politics: the electricity crisis and you.

ISBN 1 86254 606 1.

1. Electric utilities – South Australia. 2. Electric industries –
South Australia. 3. Electric power consumption – South Australia.
4. Power resources – South Australia. I. Spoehr, John.

333.7932099423

www.ajustaustralia.com

CONTENTS

Energy Efficiency, Equity and Sustainability

CHAPTER 1

Power Politics
Crisis and reform

JOHN SPOEHR

After nearly half a century under public ownership and control, the electricity industry in Australia is now subject to the influence of market principles and private interests. Over the last ten years most attempts to privatise electricity assets have failed. As a consequence, only two states in Australia have managed to sell or lease electricity assets – Victoria and South Australia. There is no immediate prospect of other states and territories doing the same. Strong community opposition and the inability to get a parliamentary majority are ensuring this for the time being. However, the struggle over the ownership and control of the industry will continue. *Power Politics* chronicles the history of one such struggle in South Australia.

Few debates have stimulated as intense community and political interest in recent times in South Australia as the privatisation of the state's electricity industry. The Liberal Government's policy backflip on privatisation was deeply unpopular in the South Australian community, with the vast majority of South Australians wanting the industry to remain publicly owned and managed. Furthermore, they were skeptical about the claimed benefits of privatisation. Community dissatisfaction with the privatisation of the Electricity Trust of South Australia (ETSA) undoubtedly contributed to the erosion of the Liberal Party's slim majority at the 9 February 2002 state election. Ultimately a Labor Government was formed with the support of the independent member for Hammond, Peter Lewis, a disgruntled former Liberal Party member.

The seeds of the electricity crisis in South Australia were sewn in

1

the early 1990s with the establishment of the National Electricity Market (NEM). The NEM offered the prospect of a more efficient electricity industry with, as a consequence, cheaper power prices. As we shall see later in this book, the NEM is unlikely to deliver on these promises. Indeed it is now clear that the new market-based system has failed so far to deliver on the promises made by the former Liberal Government.

While the sale of publicly owned electricity assets was not a requirement of the NEM, the market principles upon which the NEM was based have been used as a pretext for privatisation by a number of governments. In the face of strong community opposition, bold promises were made about the benefits of privatisation. Consumers around Australia were promised lower electricity prices and greater reliability by the architects of the National Electricity Market. South Australian households and small businesses are now bracing themselves for a very different outcome as they enter the NEM in 2003. They know that they face similar price hikes to those recently experienced by large businesses in the state. Some estimates suggest the likely initial increase facing households will be around 20% or $178 on the average power bill. Households also remember summer power blackouts in 2000 and they remain alert to the possibility that these are likely to recur. With sections of the electricity industry advocating the introduction of new power meters at a cost of $600 to each consumer, South Australian consumers were left with little doubt who the beneficiaries of the NEM and the ETSA privatisation process might be. The NEM is not working well for South Australian consumers and the ETSA privatisation has reduced the state government's influence over the NEM.

South Australians are not alone in grappling with the price crisis in the NEM. Both Queensland and New South Wales sought to delay the entry of domestic and small business consumers into the national market. Fearful of large increases in domestic power prices, they considered the introduction of price caps. However, the same options may not be available to the South Australian Government because of the ETSA privatisation. One of the perverse consequences of the privatisation of ETSA is that the contracts with new private power operators may prevent the government from introducing price caps. The only strategy for price control being seriously canvassed in South Australia has been 'price justification', a process whereby industry is asked to justify to regulators whether price increases are fair and reasonable. This is 'paper tiger' public policy, reflecting just how impotent the state government has become in the NEM.

The NEM experiment has failed the price test set by its designers, and states like South Australia which have privatised their electricity assets are relatively 'powerless' to deal with the price crisis unless fundamental reforms to the NEM are introduced. The NEM currently operates too much like a highly speculative stockmarket. This is not an appropriate model for the future development and management of the electricity industry as it is likely to perpetuate wild price fluctuations and under-investment in the development of sustainable energy-generation technologies. The Californian electricity crisis and the recent collapse of the US energy trading giant, Enron, demonstrate the inherent risks associated with over-reliance on market-based electricity systems like the NEM. The collapse of the US energy company giant, NRG Inc. in December 2002 brought this problem closer to home. NRG is the parent company of NRG Flinders which had acquired electricity generation assets in South Australia and Victoria. When NRG Inc. collapsed in the US, the South Australian subsidiary was put into voluntary administration, exposing the South Australian Government to a potential liability of up to $140 million due to a government guarantee built into the contract which NRG Flinders signed with the former Liberal Government. Not surprisingly, the new state Labor Government feared the crisis might have wider implications, so it immediately established an inquiry into all the electricity privatisation contracts struck by the previous administration.

More rather than less public accountability and engagement in the industry will be necessary to avoid such problems. The NEM will fail the fair and reasonable power price and public accountability test while market ideologues and energy speculators determine the rules governing the industry.

The threat of substantial electricity price increases and the NRG crisis are early warning signs to the government that major reform of the South Australian electricity industry will be required if wider public interest and environmental objectives are to be met. South Australia needs a strategy which integrates social, economic and environmental objectives into a comprehensive sustainable energy strategy for the state. By integrating the need for affordable energy with energy demand management and the development of renewable energy, South Australia could lead the nation in the development of a sustainable energy industry. Moreover, this industry of the future has the potential to be a major generator of new jobs and exports. The challenge for the state government is to provide the leadership to develop a policy which adopts a 'triple bottom line' approach to energy industry policy, one which focusses on affordability, energy efficiency and the need for renewable energy. An 'authority for environmentally sustainable energy' should be established to drive such reform.

To begin to meet this challenge it will be necessary to rethink the 'economics' of the electricity industry. Over-reliance on market-based economics will undermine the capacity of the government to ensure that this triple bottom line approach is realised. As noted earlier, the privatisation of the electricity industry in South Australia and its parallel participation in the National Electricity Market have raised concerns in the community about electricity pricing and system reliability. It now appears that the government has less capacity to meet social objectives like affordability and reliability, and environmental objectives such as reducing pollution and greenhouse gas emissions.

Privatisation of the electricity industry in South Australia has increased the potential for price shocks. In order to maximise proceeds from the sale of electricity assets, new generation initiatives, with the exception of Pelican Point, were not pursued vigorously by the previous state government. Since privatisation the focus of policy has been upon increasing supply through gas- and coal-fired generation capacity and interconnectors. Inadequate attention has been paid to alternative methods of matching supply and demand such as demand-side management measures designed to reduce consumption. The development of renewable sources of energy such as solar and wind power also requires much more attention.

A more rational solution which serves the public interest is needed for the development of the Australian electricity industry, one that is consumer- and environment-focussed rather than focussed on short-term speculative gains for the benefit of the energy-trading industry. 1n 1945 South Australian Premier Tom Playford took an important step down this road by establishing a royal commission into the privately run Adelaide Electric Supply Company. He was concerned that the company was too focussed on shareholders' interests: that it was seeking higher dividends while resisting the need to increase South Australia's fuel self-sufficiency and promote industrialisation. At that time the royal commission found that the public interest would be best served by nationalising the Adelaide Electric Supply Company and creating what is now known as the Electricity Trust of South Australia – ETSA. Today we are faced with similar questions about the appropriate role of government in the future development of the industry. The logic of Playford's response to this challenge in 1945 is just as compelling now – a royal commission would be both a timely and appropriate response.

A royal commission has the power and independence to help ensure a fearless and comprehensive inquiry into the Australian electricity industry and the NEM. The foremost objective of the commission would be a review of the structure and operation of the NEM and the provision of advice on the appropriate role of government to ensure fair and reasonable prices, effective demand management and sustainable generation strategies from the industry. Future generations will thank those who have the courage and vision to confront the energy policy problems and challenges this state and nation faces.

This book aims to stimulate debate on the need for fundamental reform of the electricity industry in Australia and South Australia. Understanding the origins of the public electricity industry is vital to the creation of a context where industry is more committed and open to the public interest. It is also crucial that the debate on ownership and control of the industry in the twenty-first century is not dominated by those interested in prices and profits but focussed on the many social and environmental imperatives which must be faced if we are to develop a sustainable and socially responsible energy industry for the future.

Power Politics is divided into three parts. The first part provides an overview of the origins of the public electricity industry in South Australia, the emergence of a market-based electricity system and the privatisation of the industry in South Australia. Part two attempts to demystify the NEM and offer a number of critical perspectives on its rationale and operation. Part three outlines a range of ideas for change and reform, including some lessons from overseas and locally on energy efficiency, renewable energy, low-income consumers and reform of the NEM. Importantly, this includes ideas to assist households, industry and government to use energy more efficiently, with the dual aim of reducing demand for energy and meeting environmental objectives.

The privatisation of the South Australian electricity industry is likely to remain one of the most unpopular decisions ever made by a government in South Australia. For this reason the momentum for fundamental reform is likely to grow. It may eventually prove to be as overwhelming as it was in 1945 when the premier of the day, Tom Playford, called a royal commission which led to the nationalisation of the industry in 1946. It is highly likely that the eventual privatisation by the Liberal Government in 1998 (despite their 1997 election promise not to do so) contributed to their defeat in 2002. It is also highly likely that the current Labor Government will continue to suffer the repercussions of electricity privatisation in South Australia for a long time to come. It faces the challenge of developing an energy policy which integrates social, economic and environmental objectives in order to reassert the public interest in the face of influential private interests. This is the essence of *Power Politics*.

From Public
to Private

CHAPTER 2

Nation-building, Nationalisation and ETSA

JOHN SPOEHR

Introduction

The tumultuous events culminating in the Second World War and the growing influence of Keynesian and socialist ideas upon policy-makers profoundly shaped views about the appropriate role of government in the post-war period. South Australia was not immune to these forces for change. Wartime had sharpened the need for the development of secure and reliable sources of electricity. The post-war imperative of rebuilding a civilian economy and providing housing and employment in South Australia generated momentum for greater government control over the electricity industry.

South Australian Liberal Premier Tom Playford understood the strategic importance of the industry to the industrialisation of the state. His dealings with the privately run industry led him to believe that it would not play the critical role required of it in the industrialisation process. At this time South Australia was heavily dependent upon interstate sources of black coal to fuel local electricity generators. This dependence upon interstate coal and the reluctance of the privately owned Adelaide Electric Supply Co. (AESC) to more fully exploit locally available coal at Leigh Creek frustrated Playford. When the company announced its intention to pay an increased dividend to its shareholders, Playford responded by calling a royal commission into the AESC. The commission would prove to be the vehicle he needed to forge an electricity industry more committed to the public interest in South Australia.

The context to nationalisation

Public ownership of electricity assets in Australia was widespread by the late 1930s. In this context it was not surprising that pressure mounted for nationalisation of the industry in South Australia. In the end South Australia was the last state to take this action.

The debate surrounding the nationalisation of the electricity industry in South Australia highlights an apparent political paradox – that it was a Liberal Government that brought about the nationalisation of the industry. Paradox or not, it was the particular political and economic circumstances of the time which provoked the nationalisation of the industry in 1946.

Origins and early development of the electricity industry in South Australia

While the early electricity industry in South Australia was a private undertaking, its existence depended upon government support. Electrical energy emerged as a welcome alternative to gas lighting. This new industry offered the prospect of breaking the monopoly over lighting provision held by the South Australian Gas Company (Linn 1996, p. 15). This objective appears to be the intention of the first legislation dealing with the electricity industry, the *Gas and Electric Lighting Act 1891*. By enabling local government to be a supplier of electricity, the act broke the monopoly on gas lighting provision held by the South Australian Gas Company.

The electricity industry in South Australia emerged in a practical sense at the end of the nineteenth century with the establishment in 1895 of the South Australian Electric Light and Motive Power Company Limited, a private company established under the *South Australian Companies Act*. The objective of the company was to supply electricity to the public and private sectors. With the passing of the *South Australian Electric Light and Motive Power Company Act 1897* the company was granted a franchise to supply electricity.

The act was designed to 'empower' the company to 'generate, accumulate, distribute, and supply electricity for motive power and lighting purposes, and by means of electricity, to light cities, towns, streets, docks, markets, public and private buildings and places' (Royal Commission 1946, p. 5). A range of provisions within the legislation were aimed at regulating the company's activities to ensure that the company did not operate 'exclusively in its own interests and without regard to those of the public'. To ensure fair treatment, the legislation required the company to show no 'undue preference to any local authority person or other company' (Royal Commission 1946, p. 6). Section 27 of the act enabled regulation to be made in relation to 'securing the regular and sufficient supply of electricity' and 'limiting the price to be charged'. Of particular significance is section 26 of the act which enabled 'a local authority ... after the expiration of ten years and thereafter at the end of each period of two years to purchase the whole or portion of the Company's works in its area'. The 1946 royal commission into the AESC indicated that there had been no attempt to utilise sections 26 and 27 of the 1897 act until 1932, when a committee of inquiry into electricity charges and related matters was established in accordance with section 27.

As contracts for gas lighting provided by the SA Gas Company approached expiry, a debate about the relative merits of electric and gas lighting intensified. As early as 1889, the Port Adelaide Council had indicated that electric lighting would be a 'safer' alternative (Linn 1996, p. 17). In 1897 the council signed a ten-year contract with the South Australian Electric Light and Motive Power Company to provide lighting for the area. A temporary powerhouse was built and completed by the company in 1898. By 1899 some of the streets of Port Adelaide had electric lights (ESAA 1957, p. 65). The early experiments in Port Adelaide were disappointing, largely due to the poor standard of the equipment and poor installation (Linn 1996, p. 20). The recruitment by the company of a new engineer, F.W.H. Wheadon in 1899 greatly improved this situation. New power stations were constructed in Adelaide just as the twentieth century dawned. The company returned a profit from its Adelaide powerhouse of around £4700 over the four years to 1904.

British interests and capital played a key role in the development of the electricity industry in South Australia, with the shape of the industry largely determined by decisions made in London. The directors of the South Australian Electric Light and Motive Power Company were based in London. A London-based company, the Electric Lighting and Traction Co. of Australia Limited, acquired the assets of the South Australian Electric Light and Motive Power Company in 1899. The company already had extensive interests in Australia, supplying electricity to Melbourne and Geelong (Linn 1996, p. 22). The South Australian assets of the Electric Lighting and Traction Co. of Australia were later purchased by the Adelaide Electric Supply Company (AESC) which had been incorporated for this purpose in England in 1905. The AESC was registered as a foreign company in Adelaide and was subject to the 1897 act governing the electricity industry in South Australia.

The demand for electricity grew rapidly in South Australia, rising from around 600 consumers in 1904 to around 13,000 in 1914 and 41,000 in 1922 (Linn 1996, p. 31). A new power station constructed on reclaimed land at Osborne was opened in 1923.

Reflecting the growing size and importance of the South Australian electricity industry, as well as increasing pressure for the removal of taxation on the company by both the Australian and British Governments, the AESC resolved in 1921 to shift its management from London to Adelaide. Soon after this, the 1897 act was amended to enable the company to operate in all parts of the state, although it had to seek approval via a resolution of ratepayers to operate in municipalities which had established their own generation-and-supply utilities. In practice, this enabled the AESC to establish a virtual monopoly over electricity generation and supply in South Australia. By 1926 the AESC had over 60,000 consumers and 883 employees. The onset of the Great Depression slowed but did not stop the growth of new consumers, and by 1937, the company had around 95,000 consumers. In that year it recorded a 14% increase in net revenue (Linn 1996, p. 45).

The wake of the Depression saw industrial development and jobs' growth become a political and economic imperative. The Butler Government (1927–30 and 1933–38) recognised this through the provision of infrastructure and other support to assist in the establishment of new industries in South Australia. Institutions such as ETSA and the newly created Housing Trust played a key role in this. The demand for electricity grew rapidly after the Depression, with maximum demand rising from 29,300 kW in 1935 to 63,800 kW during the war in 1943 (ESAA 1957, p. 65).

The entry of Australia into the Second World War created new imperatives for the electricity industry. Until that time the industry supported rapidly growing consumer and industrial needs. Australia's participation in the war required that it service a range of military needs as well. The war resulted in a 'phenomenal ... increase in industrial activities in South Australia' (ESAA 1957, p. 65). As indicated above, this fuelled rapid growth in demand for electricity which continued in the post-war period. By 1956 maximum demand for electricity had risen dramatically to around 250,000 kW.

State involvement in the electricity industry

South Australia was relatively late in developing an integrated public electricity system. By the mid-point of the royal commission into the AESC in 1945 there was already widespread public ownership of the electricity industry in Australia. By 1936–37 around 47% of electricity generation stations in Australia were publicly owned, while by 1937–38, 86% of electricity in Australia was generated by publicly owned utilities (Boehm 1956, p. 258). In New South Wales the figure was 76% and in Victoria it was 95%. The establishment of statutory corporations in the industry occurred as early as 1914 in Tasmania, 1918 in Victoria, 1935 in New South Wales and 1938 in Queensland.

An active role for government in the development of the electricity industry in Australia was first forged in Tasmania through the establishment of the Hydro-Electric Department. The department was charged with the responsibility for developing Tasmania's hydro-electric power system and supplying power to a number of municipalities. In this way the department played a key role in enabling the development of the mining industry in Tasmania. In 1930 the Hydro-Electric Commission was established to develop an integrated power system within the state, over time acquiring municipally owned power infrastructure which ultimately led to the development of an integrated state-owned system throughout Tasmania (Boehm 1956, p. 260).

In Victoria also, government involvement in the electricity industry was established early. A statutory authority – the State Electricity Commissioners – was set up in 1918 with the task of coordinating the development of the industry in Victoria (Boehm 1956, p. 260). The motivations for state involvement at the time were expressed by the Advisory Committee on Brown Coal which preceded the establishment of the new authority. These were:

That whether or not the State undertake the generation and distribution in bulk of electrical energy, the State should control and direct the co-ordination of all State and statutory generating and distributing schemes in Victoria, so as to ensure the adoption of standards that will admit of efficient interconnection of these schemes and the economical supply of electrical energy throughout the State. (cited in Boehm 1956, p. 260)

This recommendation had a profound influence on views about the appropriate role of government in the development of the electricity supply industry. A consensus emerged from the committee's view that the state should play a key role in the development of the industry, particularly to influence the 'pace of development' of the industry. The State Electricity Corporation took the place of the electricity authority in 1920 and by the early 1950s it provided around 98% of Victoria's electricity (Boehm 1956, p. 260).

In New South Wales the state had limited involvement in the electricity industry until 1950 when the Electricity Commission of New South Wales was established. Prior to this time the system was characterised by a range of municipally based electricity suppliers, with no overall coordination of the system. This changed in 1935 with the introduction of the *Gas and Electricity Supply Act* which required suppliers to submit development plans to an electricity advisory committee for approval. During the war years momentum grew for the development of a more integrated and coordinated system with an increase in demand for electricity along with concerns about security of supply (Boehm 1956, p. 261). This led to the establishment of the state-owned Electricity Commission of New South Wales which, through its capacity to acquire municipal power generators, came to be the provider of nearly all of the electricity requirements by the mid-1950s.

Technological advancement

A range of technical advancements in the generation and distribution of electricity made closer integration of the industry possible. With this also came the desire to ensure that the pace of integration was not impeded by the fragmented ownership structure of the industry. Initially, municipally based generation and distribution was the only option available to meet the power needs of communities. In the early years of electrification it was not economically feasible to transmit electricity over long distances. Thus municipally based generation and distribution networks were a logical outcome, given this limitation, a situation which changed with the development of new technologies and as the demand for electricity rapidly grew, particularly as a result of industrialisation.

Advances in generating technology leading to the development of larger generators made the production of electricity more efficient. As the capital costs of the development of new generating capacity came down, so also did the costs of electricity transmission. Improvements such as the pooling of reserve capacity by larger generators rather than many small ones, the capacity to improve economies of scale in the provision of power through larger generators and better integrated distribution networks, and the capacity to share risk across the system, were among key technical advances driving the development of a more integrated system (Boehm 1956, p. 263).

The role of ideas

Nationalisation of the electricity industry in South Australia gained broader theoretical legitimacy during the immediate post-Second World War period. Socialist ideas had provided a basis for this but it was the pervasive ascendancy of Keynesian economic ideas in capitalist countries throughout the world at this time that proved to be the decisive ideological driver of nationalisation in the South Australian context. The widespread adoption of Keynesian ideas provided much of the theoretical legitimacy for the pursuit of nationalisation, enabling considerable justification for public enterprise and public investment. Importantly, key advisors to Premier Playford such as Auditor General J.W. Wainwright had closely studied Keynesian ideas. Wainwright was likely to be among the first senior government officials to begin applying some of these ideas within government in Australia, ideas which provided ideological legitimacy for a policy direction which otherwise would have been regarded as socialist in origin, and indeed this is what some within Premier Playford's party feared – that government acquisition of a private company was the thin end of the socialist wedge. While this may have been the hope of some socialists at the time, the nationalisation of the industry in South Australia was, as we shall discover, firmly rooted in capitalist rather than socialist objectives. Having said that, socialist ideas were important and influential in shaping the ownership of utilities in the post-war Australian context. Like Keynsianism, socialism could provide the ideological legitimacy for nationalisation of the industry, but only within the framework of a radical program of public ownership of the means of production. The key point to make about the role of ideas in shaping debates about public versus private ownership in the immediate post-war period is that the ascendancy of Keynesian and socialist ideas created a political space where neoliberal economic views about the sanctity of private ownership, were for a time, in retreat.

Labor and nationalisation

The Labour Party argued for nationalisation of the electricity industry in line with its policy platform. During a debate about the future of the electricity industry in 1943, a Labour member in the House of Assembly proposed a case for public ownership of the industry. He argued that public ownership would enable government to place the public interest ahead of shareholder interests, helping to ensure wider social and economic benefits for the larger community.

We know very well that our railways have greatly helped to develop South Australia. In the same way waterworks have assisted in opening up the country. I do not look upon either of those great projects as a means of making profits, but as instruments for rendering service to the people. If we had sources of electrical energy doing the same thing it would be well worthwhile ... The sooner we decide that all public utilities shall be controlled by the State for the benefit of the people, instead of for those who draw dividends, the better it will be for everyone.

The industrialisation imperative

Following the Depression, the South Australian Government adopted a policy designed to balance primary and secondary industry in South Australia, and a great industrial development commenced. This, coupled with a progressive policy on domestic electrification by the Company including the introduction of the 'Adelect' Hiring Scheme in 1935, resulted in a great increase in the demand for electricity. (ESAA 1957, p. 64)

The nationalisation of the electricity industry in South Australia was linked to the political and economic imperative of industrialisation in the wake of the 1930s Depression. The widespread unemployment and poverty during this period had a profound influence on local politics. The necessity for action to deal with the crisis could hardly be ignored. Indeed as Linn (1996, p. 51) suggests, it is likely that: 'All were staggered by the depth of the Depression and the catastrophe that loomed for the State if something was not done to reform its economy'. For some it appeared that capitalism was on the verge of collapse as Marx had predicted in the 'Communist Manifesto'. Socialist ideas had by this time played a key role in the transformations of Russia and China. Furthermore, it was likely that socialist ideas would gain wider acceptance in the context of a prolonged crisis in capitalist countries. While the prospect of a socialist transformation did not represent any real threat to the established 'liberal' order in South Australia, socialist ideas and organisations did create new political spaces for a debate about a broader role for government.

In South Australia industrial unrest and the rise of the Labour Party as a political force generated momentum for reform rather than for a radical transformation, placing pressure on government to take a more activist role in industrial development. Keynesian ideas provided a circuit-breaker for the crisis of capitalism by offering a 'third way' between laissez-faire capitalism and socialism, given subsequent political expression in strategies like the American New Deal which gave legitimacy to state-sponsored public works and industrialisation initiatives in Australia. While few policy-makers in South Australia appreciated the theoretical basis for these, some like J.W. Wainwright had made the effort to read Keynes' *The General Theory of*

Employment, Interest and Money. This knowledge is likely to have been important in informing the advice that Wainwright provided to Premiers Butler and Playford.

The Depression had left South Australia and its economy in poor condition. There was insufficient revenue to cover public-sector salaries and there were mounting liabilities. The necessity for implementing strategies to promote industrial development and jobs growth was great.

The Butler Government began a process of promoting industrialisation by reducing company tax to the lowest rate in the country and by providing specific support to firms willing to locate to, or expand in South Australia. In exchange for BHP (Broken Hill Proprietary Company) agreeing to the construction of a blast furnace in Whyalla, the Butler Government provided the company with various concessions, security of its mineral lease and a low rate of royalties payable to the government (Linn 1996, p. 51). To ensure that BHP had access to adequate water supplies, the government gave a commitment to extending a pipeline from the Murray River to Whyalla. A similar strategy had been used when it agreed to provide a package of support to British Tube Mills.

After Premier Richard Butler resigned his state seat in a failed attempt to secure a federal seat in Parliament in 1938, he was replaced as Premier of South Australia by Tom Playford. Playford continued to build on the Butler Government's approach to industrial development. Significantly, the strategy of promoting industrialisation depended upon the development of a reliable and cost-effective electricity industry.

By the early 1940s the extent to which the AESC could serve the industrial development objectives of the government emerged as a significant question. The main issues of concern related to access to secure coal supplies, along with the dividend, costs and charging policies of the AESC.

The Leigh Creek coal debate
The need for greater reliability of coal supplies and the prospect of achieving this objective through the use of locally available Leigh

Creek coal became a key issue of debate between the state government and the AESC.

Since its establishment, the electricity industry in South Australia had been dependent upon interstate sources of coal. The generating plants were designed exclusively to use high-grade black coal sourced from Newcastle. When industrial action disrupted the availability of this coal and the AESC was forced to purchase supplies from England, security of supply became a key issue (Linn 1996, p. 52). Moreover, Australia's participation in the Second World War along with coal shortages served to sharpen concern about the need for more secure supplies of coal. A ten-week strike in the NSW coalfields in 1940 further reinforced these concerns.

The necessity for a reliable local source of coal was also driven by rapid growth in both consumer and industrial demand for electricity in South Australia during the post-Depression period. Growth in the demand for electricity was a function of a number of factors, including a growing population, the relative cost-effectiveness of electricity by comparison with gas, the development of new electrical appliances and hire schemes to promote their use, and industrial expansion. Moreover, due to a dependence upon interstate and overseas sources of coal electricity, prices were relatively higher in South Australia. In this context the pursuit of a local alternative supply was of great strategic significance as lower-cost fuel offered the prospect of lower electricity prices.

Early investigations of Leigh Creek indicated an extensive deposit of sub-bituminous coal. This lower-grade source of coal could not be burnt in existing plant without additional refinement and modifications.

Although initially suggesting that the state government make use of Leigh Creek coal as an 'emergency source of fuel', the AESC did not support extensive use of it in the industry (Linn 1996, p. 58), consistently arguing that it was not economical. This position saw the company in conflict with the state government which was eager, despite the AESC's views, to make use of Leigh Creek coal to overcome problems of secure access to coal. Just after the outbreak of the Second World War the concerns of Premier Tom Playford and the state government in relation to coal supplies were clearly evident as a former Manager of the Leigh Creek mine later reflected.

In 1940 the Premier became deeply concerned with the lack of supplies of coal for public utilities and industrial requirements. Reserve stocks had fallen far below the quantity considered to be a safe margin. Despite efforts to improve the situation it had not been possible to build up stocks to any extent even with the curtailment of public utilities – this being due principally to shipping difficulties and the increased demand of the other States. The Government was forced to give serious considera-tion to the matter in order to remedy the position and also from the aspect of making South Australia independent, or partly so, for its coal supplies. [Gilbert Poole cited in Linn 1996, p. 55]

It appears that Premier Playford had a strong personal commit-ment to ensuring that Leigh Creek coal became the major source of fuel for electricity generation in South Australia. Playford applied considerable pressure on the AESC to pursue this objective (Linn 1996, p. 56). The AESC was not persuaded, arguing that Leigh Creek Coal was 'relatively untested' and too expensive to use. The impasse came to a head in 1942 when Playford introduced legislation requiring the use of the coal. The bill was hotly debated and subse-quently passed once it had been amended in the Legislative Council, and the critical clause requiring the mining and use of Leigh Creek coal removed. Playford and the state government persisted, appointing a committee to review the desirability or otherwise of a new power station (at Port Augusta) along with matters relating to the extension of electricity supply in metropolitan areas (Committee of Inquiry into Electricity Supply in South Australia 1943, p. 5). Importantly the committee was required to determine whether the new power station was in the public interest. It defined the public interest in relation to electricity supply as: '(A) Security – (In the form of reliability, continuity, and sufficiency of supply; and (B) Economy – (In the form of the cheapest supply to consumers)'. In its expanded definition of what constitutes the 'public interest', the committee reinforced the state government's views about the broader strategic importance of developing local sources of fuel. Significantly, it opened up the possibility of a greater role for government, pointing to the need for a greater level of coordination of the industry.

The committee recommended that further research be undertaken to determine the full potential of Leigh Creek coal and other locally available fuel sources. It found that Leigh Creek coal was suitable for use in steam-generation plants and it identified options for its immediate use in conjunction with New South Wales coal.

The committee of inquiry's findings regarding the use of Leigh Creek coal were significant for Premier Playford in that they established that, while the cost of using local coal would be greater, there were broader benefits to be derived from reducing South Australia's dependence upon interstate sources. Not surprisingly, the AESC did not welcome this conclusion or the prospect of a new electricity coordinating authority (Linn 1996, p. 60).

As a result of the inquiry, a bill to establish an Electricity Commission was introduced by Premier Playford on 7 December 1943. In arguing the case for the commission, Playford drew attention to the lack of electricity services in rural areas and the failure to develop local fuel resources for the industry.

... if members take a general view of electricity supplies in South Australia they will see that the service has not extended appreciably to many rural districts ... Scant regard seems to have been paid to approximately half of our population which is resident outside the metropolitan area ... we have to depend on a long overseas voyage for our coal and oil supplies which, during war-time, is an extremely serious position to be in.

Premier Playford challenged the AESC's dismissal of the committee's report, arguing that there were 'no grounds whatever' for the criticisms levelled at the report by the AESC chairperson. The debate between Playford and the AESC intensified, with each party challenging the other about the relative merits of Leigh Creek coal. Playford launched a strong attack on the AESC's claims, claiming that Leigh Creek coal, through practical demonstrations in powerhouses, was proving to be a viable alternative fuel.

While Premier Playford had become convinced of the wisdom of making greater use of Leigh Creek coal, this viewpoint was not shared by the AESC which regarded extensive use of local coal as counter to its financial interests. A very public deadlock had been reached between the AESC and the state government which Playford sought to break in his favour. The establishment of an Electricity Commission in 1943 offered the prospect of advancing the case for Leigh Creek. Soon after the commission became operational, Premier Playford asked two of its members, H.T.M Angwin and F.H. Harrison to investigate overseas facilities which used sub-bituminous coal like that found at Leigh Creek. In November 1944, Angwin and Harrison provided a progress report on the outcomes of extensive investigations in the United States and Canada. They reported on successful use of sub-bituminous coals in Canada, demonstrating that Leigh Creek coal could be successfully burnt. With this information Premier Playford was in a stronger position to advance his case.

Pace of electrification

There were other sources of tension between the Playford Government and the AESC which helped to propel the state government towards acquisition of the state's electricity assets. Among these was the concern that the AESC was not driving the electrification of the state as fast as was desired, and that significant parts of South Australia were not adequately catered for. This concern was reinforced by a view within the government that the AESC's duty to shareholders conflicted with the broader public need for electrification to be extended throughout the entire state. In this context there was heightened concern about attempts by the AESC to increase dividends returned to shareholders.

Shareholder interests and the public interest

A key turning point in events leading to the nationalisation of the electricity industry appears to a recommendation by the AESC Board to convert 8% of preference shares to ordinary shares and issue £1,125,000 of new ordinary shares (Linn 1996, p. 61). The proposal was seen by J.W. Wainwright, South Australian Auditor General, as benefitting shareholders at the expense of consumers. This motivated

Wainwright to suggest regulation of the AESC's operations and pricing policies. In response, the AESC sought to negotiate a deal with Premier Playford, brokering the option of a royal commission should the company believe that it was disadvantaged by the proposed legislation. Through its request for a royal commission, the AESC had set in motion a series of events that would soon result in its demise.

The royal commission into the AESC

The Royal Commission into the Adelaide Electric Supply Company was established on 15 February 1945 and comprised three people – G.W. Reed, an Adelaide Supreme Court Judge, Professor A.L. Campbell an engineer and nominee of the AESC, and J.W. Wainwright, the South Australian Auditor General and nominee of Premier Playford. The royal commission had very broad terms of reference. It was charged with the responsibility of inquiring into and reporting upon the supply of electricity by the AESC and all matters related to the electricity industry in South Australia. The royal commission handed down its findings to the government in September 1945, recommending that the assets of the AESC be acquired and that the shareholders be adequately compensated for their losses. Premier Playford welcomed the result and on 11 October 1945, he introduced a bill into the South Australian Parliament, the *Electricity Trust of South Australia Act* to nationalise the industry. After considerable resistance from within his own party, Premier Playford managed to secure the one vote that was necessary to pass the legislation. On 9 April 1946 the legislation was passed in the Legislative Council of the South Australian Parliament. The new publicly owned and controlled industry came into being on 1 September 1946.

While it did not find any major fault with the AESC, the royal commission had outlined a range of concerns relating to security of supply, the pace of electrification in regional areas, power costs, industry development, shareholder interests and the financial advantages of public ownership. Combined, these concerns amounted to a powerful case for public ownership of the industry.

Shareholder interests

The nationalisation of South Australia's electricity industry was in part a product of an irreconcilable conflict between shareholder interests and the public interest. The royal commission pointed to a 'lack of restraint by the AESC to restrain dividends and therefore prices', also noting that:

An adequate supply of electricity at reasonable rates is of the utmost importance to the community particularly for the development of industry. The interests of the public in this regard have so far been largely at the discretion of the directors of the Company. Its [the Adelaide Electric Supply Company] claim that the public interest has been and will continue to be studied tends to conflict with the directors' duty to shareholders. [Royal Commission 1946]

Moreover, the royal commission argued 'the need for electricity charges to be set at rates which support local industry development'.

Financial advantages

Among the more pragmatic reasons for nationalisation emerging from the royal commission was the claim that public ownership would reduce the costs of electricity enterprises because a public utility would be exempt from taxation and have access to lower rates of interest, normally available to state enterprises. The financial advantages of public ownership were specified in the following terms.

One of the large items in the Company's annual expenditure is for company taxation. For the year ending 31 August, 1944, it was about £200,000, and for several years past it has been in the region of that amount. If this liability did not exist tariffs could be substantially reduced. The average price for 1944 – 1.66d per k.w. hour – would have been .24d lower if the undertaking had been free from taxation.

The average rate for interest and dividends paid by the Company last year on debentures and share capital, and inclusive of reserves invested in the business, was 4.69%. The corresponding figure for the State Electricity Commission of Victoria was 3.37% ...

Over the last 24 years the Company has paid £5,174,721 in dividends and interest. If it had obtained its capital at Treasury rates over this period a saving in interest and dividends of £1,370,712 would have resulted which would have been available for the purpose of reducing tariffs and/or strengthening reserves. [Royal Commission 1946]

The reluctance of the privately owned Adelaide Electric Supply Company to make use of Leigh Creek coal reserves for power generation and its failure to contain dividends to shareholders and accelerate the electrification of regional South Australia combined to convince Premier Tom Playford that broad industrial and social objectives would be best met through public ownership of the industry. Playford concluded that the only effective means of ensuring that electricity infrastructure could be utilised as a tool to advance South Australia's social and economic development lay in public ownership.

For Playford, public control over electricity provision was an essential prerequisite for the industrialisation of South Australia. Under private control, electrification of the state was proceeding slowly, and industry needs were not being met. Playford regarded electricity provision as a 'natural monopoly' where the best interests of the state were served through public ownership. This would ultimately enable him to provide the necessary electricity infrastructure to support the development of the 'passenger motor vehicle' and mining industries in South Australia. It would also ensure that regional South Australia had access to affordable power supplies since private providers saw the electrification of country areas as unprofitable. Playford and his contemporaries claimed a longer-term view of what was profitable and in the public interest.

The establishment of ETSA

The *Electricity Trust of South Australia Act* was proclaimed on 30 August 1946. On 1 September the trust assumed the assets of the Adelaide Electric Supply Company. In the following year the trust acquired the Onkaparinga Electricity Supply Company and in 1948 it took over the Mid-North Electricity Company (ESAA 1957, p. 65). The Electricity Trust of South Australia continued to acquire the assets of a range of small regional electricity companies in its role as the provider of electricity throughout the state and would play a key role in the development of South Australia for over half a century.

References

Boehm, E A 1956, 'Ownership and control of the electricity supply industry in Australia', *The Economic Record*, XXXII (November).

Committee of Enquiry into the Electricity Supply in South Australia 1943, *Report*, Government Press, Adelaide.

ESAA (Electricity Supply Association of Australia) 1957, *Some of the features of public electricity supply in Australia*, Melbourne.

Linn, R 1996, *ETSA – The story of electricity in South Australia*, Openbook Publishers, Adelaide.

Royal Commission (Royal Commission into Adelaide Electric Supply Company) 1946, *Report*, Adelaide.

South Australia, House of Assembly 1943, *Debates*, Adelaide.

CHAPTER 3

Market Power

The privatisation of the
South Australian electricity industry

JOHN SPOEHR

Introduction

Bold promises were made in 1998 by the Olsen Liberal State Government in a desperate attempt to win public and parliamentary support for the privatisation of the Electricity Trust of South Australia (ETSA). To distinguish the rhetoric from the reality we need to review the circumstances leading to the privatisation and the claims and counter-claims made throughout the ETSA debate. We start with the extraordinary policy backflip the Olsen Government made after it was re-elected in 1997.

Privatisation – the policy backflip

Soon after being re-elected for a second term of government in October 1997, the Premier, John Olsen, announced that, contrary to previous commitments, the government would privatise the state's electricity industry. This was seen as a major policy backflip given pre-election claims that it would retain ETSA in public ownership. The first signs of a change in the government's public position came on 3 September, just four weeks before the 1997 state election when the new Infrastructure Minister, Graham Ingerson, failed to rule out the possibility of privatising ETSA. However, it is clear that the government was considering options for privatisation of the electricity industry as early as December 1995. At this time the Electricity Reform Cabinet Committee directed the Electricity Sector

Reform Unit (ESRU), to 'assess the feasibility of establishing a joint venture with private and public sector partners to own assets of ETSA Transmission and to outsource the management and function of the business entity' (Electricity Sector Reform Unit 1996, p. 1). The composition of the project team established for the task indicated that key government agencies and ministers were actively engaged in the process. The ESRU report argued that a net gain of around $34 million would flow from the part sale of the transmission business of ETSA. It arrived at this conclusion admitting that it had not investigated 'alternative structural arrangements for ETSA'.

While options for the privatisation of ETSA were being explored by the government and ETSA early in 1995, the government did enter into an arrangement which foreshadowed its commitment to privatisation. In August 1997 it signed a $1 billion, 23-year lease of ETSA's transmission assets to a US-based financier, Edison Capital. While ETSA would retain operational control over the assets and an option to regain full control after the expiry of the lease, the deal was indicative of growing momentum within ETSA and the government for privatisation of electricity assets.

In seeking the government's endorsement of the lease of ETSA's transmission assets, the acting managing director of ETSA Corporation presented a number of privatisation options for the consideration of the government. These included part-privatisation of ETSA (Transmission Corporation) through a share float. It is likely that this position emerged from advice provided by the investment house, Schroders, which was commissioned in February 1997 by the ETSA chairperson, Mike Janes, and managing director, Clive Armour, to provide it with advice on future ownership options.

Senior members of the government were aware of and directly involved in reviewing the work undertaken by Schroders (Janes 1998a). The Premier, John Olsen and Mike Janes met with Schroders on 6 June 1997 while the Deputy Premier, Graham Ingerson was provided with a further briefing in Melbourne on 18 July 1997. The work undertaken by Schroders continued throughout 1997 despite the government's repeated claims that it had no plans to privatise ETSA.

Correspondence between ETSA and the government demonstrates that senior ministers supported the investigation and were briefed regarding its progress on regular occasions (Janes 1998a). After the 1997 election further briefings on work undertaken by Schroders were given to the new Government Business Enterprise Minister, Michael Armitage, and the Premier, John Olsen, by Mike Janes. Janes advised Armitage on 17 December that the ETSA Board would be 'reaching a conclusion' regarding the issues raised by the Schroders investigation (Janes 1998a).

In January 1998 the ETSA Board forwarded its conclusions to the government, recommending that ETSA be fully privatised through a share float. A letter from the chairperson of ETSA, Mike Janes, to the Government Business Enterprise Minister, Michael Armitage, recommended: 'that the privatisation of ETSA should be pursued immediately and that it should be implemented through a float of 100% of the shares of ETSA' (Janes 1998b). A fallback position involving a partial float of 49% of ETSA was also included in the proposal.

The capacity of ETSA to manage risks effectively in the emerging National Electricity Market (NEM) emerged as a serious question after ETSA reported that it faced a $96.8 million write-down arising from an arrangement it had with the Osborne Power Station for the supply of power. In its 1996–97 annual report released in December 1998, ETSA indicated that it would be paying more than necessary for power from Osborne given the emergence of cheaper sources of power. The Infrastructure Minister, Graham Ingerson, claimed that he had only learnt of the write-down after the ETSA annual report had been tabled in State Parliament. This claim was disputed in State Parliament by the Leader of the Labor Opposition, Mike Rann, who alleged that Ingerson must have known about the write-down for a number of months, as he had indicated this in earlier statements in parliament.

While knowledge of the ETSA write-down was a source of political embarrassment to the government, this situation did add credibility to the government's early arguments about the risks associated with operating in a competitive electricity market.

The privatisation decision

On Tuesday 17 February 1998, the Premier, John Olsen, announced in State Parliament that the government had decided to sell ETSA and Optima. He indicated that the government was also considering the sale of a range of other assets, including the TAB, the Lotteries Commission, WorkCover, the Motor Accident Commission, HomeStart and the Ports Corporation. Premier Olsen claimed that it had always been his 'stated intention to retain ETSA and Optima but risks associated with joining the National Electricity Market (NEM) had led to his change of mind'.

There were two main reasons given by the Premier for the policy reversal. Broadly these were that the state government was obliged to sell ETSA to eliminate a range of 'massive' risks to taxpayers associated with South Australia's entry into the NEM and because there was no other way of making South Australia 'debt free'. The Premier claimed that he had only become aware of the 'ramifications of the national electricity market' after the release of the annual report of the Auditor General in December 1997. He argued that the report indicated that the risks associated with retaining ETSA in public ownership had substantially increased in the context of the establishment of the NEM and that the state government should, and could eliminate these risks through privatisation. He also argued that the report indicated that South Australia risked losing up to $2 billion in payments due to National Competition Policy (NCP) arrangements. A further, but unrelated, argument was that current public debt levels compromised the capacity of the government to 'balance the budget' and 'put money into essential services such as health and education'. He also argued that it was essential to substantially accelerate public debt reduction even though, at the time, public debt had declined from around $9 billion after the State Bank crisis to around $7.4 billion. The Premier claimed the interest payments on this debt were around $2 million per day.

In making the sale announcement, Premier Olsen evoked the powerful image of the 1991 State Bank crisis. On the day after the announcement he continued with this theme by drawing direct parallels between the circumstances preceding the State Bank crisis and those currently confronting ETSA. Just as financial deregulation had increased the risks faced by the State Bank, so had National Competition Policy and the creation of the NEM increased the risks faced by ETSA. To avoid similar consequences, he argued that the sale of ETSA was the only effective way to manage these risks and the only financially responsible course of action to take.

The Premier found further justification for the sale of ETSA in a report prepared by Alan Moran of the Institute of Public Affairs, a conservative economic think-tank based in Melbourne. The report urged the state government to 'move quickly to privatise its electricity supply', arguing that 'privatisation would prevent the state's tax-payers from being exposed to risk if competitive pressures reduced prices and profits in the electricity market'. Moran argued that privatisation would result in improved efficiency and net benefits to the state budget. The Premier also referred to comments made by Graham Scott, director of the SA Centre for Economic Studies, reported in the *Advertiser*. Scott claimed that 'the South Australian industry will be hard put to compete when the national grid is fully developed … and the ability to sell into other States will be very limited … ETSA's value on the marketplace is a lot more likely to decline over the next couple of years than it is to go up'.

The sense of crisis and urgency contained in the Premier's 17 February announcement was sustained over following days with claims that the 'sale of assets was essential to protect the state from bankruptcy and to protect services such as schools and hospitals'. The sale, he argued, would help to avoid the introduction of 'options such as death duties'.

Early polling of public reaction to the sale by two television stations indicated strong opposition to the sale. Around 92% of 3106 callers to a Channel 7 poll were opposed to the sale, as were around 87% of 3688 callers to a Channel 9 poll. This high level of public opposition would be sustained throughout the course of the ETSA sale debate.

The state government's campaign to sell ETSA was damaged by news on 20 February 1998, of a blackout in Auckland, New Zealand. The blackout forced the closure of industry and services throughout the city. It was widely believed that the blackout was caused by privatisation even though the Auckland electricity system, Mercury

Energy was publicly owned. As the news broke in South Australia, the crisis raised fears in the community that privatisation of ETSA would result in a similar outcome. The obvious parallel between the electricity industries in South Australia and Auckland was that they were both corporatised and substantial workforce downsizing had taken place in both utilities. Mercury Energy had halved its workforce over the three years to 1998.

While the state government's early arguments for the sale focussed on risks associated with keeping the utility in public ownership, the government subsequently argued the benefits of the sale to different constituencies. At a business luncheon attended by over 400 business people, the Premier outlined a number of priority areas for new expenditure if ETSA were sold. He indicated that if the sale went ahead, the government would provide funds for a new emergency services radio communications network, additional computers for schools and a cap on school fees. The financial benefits of the sale were also a key feature of the Premier's argument. He claimed that the sale of ETSA and Optima would result in an improvement in South Australia's credit rating, leading to 'savings of millions of dollars in interest payments'. A carrot-and-stick approach characterised the Premier's speech. While offering the prospect of new funding for public services, he also warned that the assets must be sold quickly, in particular suggesting that the value of South Australia's electricity assets would be significantly reduced if the assets were not put on the market before those of New South Wales, even though there was no immediate prospect of the NSW assets being sold.

Just one week after it announced it would sell ETSA, the state government embarked on a substantial publicity campaign to generate support for its decision. On 21 March 1998, the Premier argued the government's case for the sale on prime-time television, including Channels 7, 9 and 10. This was part of a $330,000 pro-sale campaign, nicknamed 'Project Crocodile'. The campaign included the distribution of a leaflet to all South Australian households, newspaper advertisements and an information hotline. It focussed largely on the risks of retaining ETSA in public ownership, with the Premier, John Olsen, echoing a variation of Margaret Thatcher's now-famous dictum, 'There is no alternative'.

There were soon challenges to the government's claims about the level of risk associated with ETSA under public ownership. Central to the government's arguments was a claim that the Auditor General had indicated that the state risked losing $1 billion in competition policy payments if reforms to the electricity industry were found to not conform with National Competition Policy (NCP). The government claimed that advice about such risks was not available prior to the 1997 state election. It is evident, however, that some of the Premier's closest advisors had access to a draft copy of the annual report at least six months before the state government announced its decision to sell ETSA. In particular the draft report was forwarded to the head of Premier and Cabinet, Ian Kowalick in July, 1997 (*Advertiser*, 25 February 1998, p. 19). Indeed the draft report was circulated to at least seven agencies at this time, according to the Auditor General, Ken McPherson (South Australia, House of Assembly 1998). The Premier claimed that he had no prior knowledge of the Auditor General's report until it was released.

Whatever the veracity of the Premier's claims, it is implausible that senior members of the state government were not aware of the risks associated with non-compliance with NCP. These risks were widely known by the end of 1998. Indeed, the Auditor General had drawn attention to such risks as early as 1996 in his annual report. He acknowledged that information about the potential risks relating to non-compliance with NCP would have been widely available a number of years prior to the release of his 1997 annual report.

The question of whether or not the state government had prior knowledge of the issues raised in the Auditor General's 1997 report obscures more critical issues relating to the extent to which the risks identified were a legitimate basis for the government's decision to privatise ETSA. The Auditor General's report indicated that there was no threat to competition policy payments, given that requirements specified under NCP had been met in order to activate the first NCP payments. The risks identified by the Auditor General were well understood within the public sector and strategies to manage these had been in place for some time. There was, in reality, no real or immediate threat to competition policy payments.

In claiming that retaining ETSA in public ownership would risk the loss of competition payments, the Premier had also argued that the value of ETSA would fall dramatically if it were not sold soon. He based his claim on a secret study undertaken by a consortium of consultants, including Troughton Swier and Associates, Credit Suisse First Boston and KPMG. He told Parliament that 'independent research ... states that the value of our power assets could drop by up to 50%'. This claim was likely to have been based on the shaky assumption that the NSW Government was likely to sell its publicly owned electricity industry. If this were to occur prior to the sale of ETSA, then the sale price of ETSA would, in all probability be reduced.

The Premier raised the stakes in the ETSA sale debate on 15 March 1998 when he warned that a $183 levy on top of existing electricity bills would be imposed if ETSA was not sold (*Advertiser*, 3 March 1998, p. 16). He blamed this on the Labor Party's opposition to the sale and linked the levy directly to the Labor Opposition Leader by calling it a 'Rann tax'.

The initial responses to the government's decision to sell ETSA were divergent, with business and electricity industry interests backing the proposal, while unions, community organisations, the Labor Opposition and the wider community largely opposed it. Importantly, the government did not appear to have sufficient support within the parliament to pass the necessary legislation required to privatise the electricity industry.

The parliamentary process begins
The state government wasted little time testing its sale proposal out in State Parliament. It introduced legislation to privatise ETSA into the parliament on 18 March 1998 and was immediately confronted by the reality that it would have to win additional support to pass the sale legislation in the Legislative Council. To succeed, the government would have to either win the support of the Australian Democrats and Independent No Pokies MP, Nick Xenophon, or failing this, persuade two Labor members to defect. These options seemed implausible at the time. Initially it appeared that opposition to the sale by the Australian Democrats would thwart the government's objectives.

To support its case for the sale, the state government commis-

sioned former state Auditor General Tom Sheridan to provide a
report on the fiscal impact of the sale. The findings of his report were
made public on 22 March 1998. Sheridan argued that: 'combined
sale prices in excess of $4 billion could well have a significant
favourable net impact on the State Budget' (Sheridan 1998, p. 8). He
claimed that a $4 billion sale price would produce net budgetary
savings of $29 million and a $6 billion sale price would produce
savings of around $148 million. If the sale did not go ahead he
warned that the State Budget would 'blow out by up to $123 million
in four years'. Sheridan indicated that he had not undertaken an
independent analysis of the likely impact of the proposed sale; indeed
his conclusions were derived from work undertaken by Treasury,
the Auditor General and by the consortium of consultants engaged
by the state government. He acknowledged that he had 'not been
able to undertake separate assessments or to test the veracity of
factual information obtained from these sources'.

Effectively, the government's financial argument for the sale
reduced to a simple claim: that the sale of ETSA would eliminate the
estimated $2 million in interest per day that was currently being paid
on state debt. This claim was repeated regularly throughout the
ETSA sale debate. However, it did not go unchallenged.

One challenge came from a former general manager of ETSA,
Bruce Dinham. In a letter to the editor of the *Advertiser* he argued
that privatisation would result in increased electricity prices and the
likelihood of increased taxes to compensate for the loss of revenue
from ETSA. The United Trades and Labour Council of South
Australia and a number of unions concerned about the proposed sale
of ETSA commissioned the University of Adelaide's, Centre for
Labour Research to analyse the Sheridan report and provide a cri-
tique of the government's sale arguments. The report, prepared by
John Spoehr from the Centre for Labour Research and Professor
John Quiggin, from the Australian National University reviewed
arguments surrounding the level of risk associated with continued
public ownership, and provided an alternative analysis of the likely
fiscal impact of the sale (Quiggin & Spoehr 1998). The report
concluded that Sheridan had failed to include retained earnings
in the calculation of total earnings of the enterprise, resulting in an

underestimation of earnings and undervaluation of the assets. Correcting for the omission of retained earnings indicated that a sale price in excess of $7 billion was necessary to break even. The report also reviewed the government's arguments concerning the level of risk that taxpayers were allegedly exposed to. In line with the Auditor General's conclusions regarding risk, the report indicated that there was no specific risk to the competition payments and the risks of participation in the NEM were manageable (Quiggin & Spoehr 1998, pp. 6–9).

When these claims were released in April 1998 they received considerable publicity, attracting strong criticism from the Treasurer in parliament who attempted to discredit the authors of the report by claiming their analysis was 'full of errors and inaccuracies'. In particular, he claimed that the fiscal analysis was flawed because it failed to take account of the abolition of the statutory sales levy on ETSA. The analysis did in fact take account of this matter (Quiggin & Spoehr 1998, p. 17).

The government wasted no time appointing a team of advisers to support the sale process. Early in April 1998 the state government announced that it had produced a shortlist of consultants to manage the sale of ETSA. A number of consortiums comprising high-profile international financial institutions proposed bids to manage the sale. The contract to manage the ETSA sale was ultimately awarded to the Morgan Stanley consortium.

Soon after the consultants were appointed it appeared that the government would have great difficulty in getting support for the sale in the Legislative Council. As noted earlier, the Australian Democrats indicated that they were unlikely to support the sale. In a detailed response to the government, the Democrats refuted the government's claims about the risks associated with competition payments and entry to the NEM. The Democrats particularly challenged the government's claim that a sale price of $4 billion would result in a net financial benefit to the State Budget. Drawing on Quiggin and Spoehr (1998), they argued that it was necessary for the state government to obtain at least $7 billion to ensure a net financial benefit to the state.

The Australian Democrats formally outlined their opposition to the sale of ETSA on 25 June 1998. Deputy Leader of the Democrats Sandra Kanck argued that the state government's sale case was based on 'deception, exaggeration and rubbery figures'. While they gained some support for their position from a key lower house independent MP, Rory McEwen, they were heavily criticised by Professor Cliff Walsh and the Chamber of Commerce and Industry. The Democrats' decision shifted the focus of public attention to Nick Xenophon, whose vote the ETSA sale proposal now depended upon.

Like the Australian Democrats, the Labor Party argued that there was no imperative arising from the NCP and the NEM to sell ETSA. Furthermore, Opposition Leader Mike Rann argued that there would be significant losses flowing from privatisation, particularly the loss of revenue flowing from ETSA to the State Budget.

The ETSA sale debate moved into more difficult terrain for the state government, when the Deputy Premier, Graham Ingerson, was forced to resign after being found guilty by the Privileges Committee of State Parliament of misleading parliament in relation to his knowledge of the $96 million write-down of ETSA. Under increasing pressure from Labor, the Democrats and Independents, he was forced to resign to avoid a no-confidence motion being successfully moved against him in parliament. Importantly, this decision appears to have been heavily influenced by No Pokies MP Nick Xenophon's public announcement a few days earlier that he would, 'find it difficult to support the sale of ETSA unless the Premier acts on the findings' of the Privileges Committee investigation into Ingerson.

With an impasse created by the rejection of the sale by the Democrats the government announced that it was considering the possibility of holding a referendum on the sale proposal if the legislation continued to be blocked in the upper house. It was highly unlikely that the government would pursue such an outcome given widespread community opposition to the sale of ETSA at the time. The main motivation for proposing a referendum appears to be an attempt to influence Nick Xenophon, who had initially proposed the idea of a referendum, but was yet to announce his final position regarding the sale.

A detailed plan for the sale of ETSA was released by the state government on 30 June 1998. The plan included a 'commitment to a 5-year freeze on average consumer prices, environmental standards for power generators and job protection for electricity workers'. It also made provision for the separation of various ETSA functions, including the division of Optima into three generating companies and the division of ETSA into generation, distribution and retail companies.

Just as Nick Xenophon prepared to announce his position on the ETSA sale, Labor MLC, Terry Cameron gave some early indications that he was sympathetic to the government's sale proposal. In a lengthy speech in Parliament on 23 July 1998 Cameron stated that, based on his analysis of the arguments, 'it would be in the best interests of South Australia and its people for ETSA to be sold'. He argued that there must be particularly 'compelling reasons' for the sale of ETSA given that the Labor NSW Government was considering privatisation of its electricity industry. The likelihood of Terry Cameron voting with the government to support the sale of ETSA appeared remote, particularly given that it would result in his expulsion from the Labor Party, but disappointment surrounding the direction of his career within the Labor Party may have provided some of the motivation for doing so.

As events unfolded, Cameron's determination to support the sale became clear. On 5 August, 1998 he said that he was 'prepared to be expelled from the party and cross the floor to vote for the ETSA sale'. Furthermore, he regarded the sale of ETSA as 'the most important decision facing the state in his lifetime'. On 11 August, Cameron proclaimed his support for the sale, arguing that, after the Labor Party won the next election, it would, 'inherit a nightmare if ETSA is not sold'. Comments that same day by MLC Trevor Crothers indicated that Terry Cameron was not the only Labor MP willing to support the sale of ETSA. Crothers indicated that: 'he would have had considerable difficulty not supporting the sale of ETSA' if Premier Olsen had declared the government's support for the sale of ETSA prior to the 1997 election.

The significance of Terry Cameron's decision increased when No Pokies MP Nick Xenophon announced that he would oppose the sale unless a referendum were held on the issue. This shifted the focus on to Trevor Crothers. As indicated earlier, the government was unlikely to support a referendum given widespread community opposition to the sale. In this situation the government needed the support of Crothers to pass its sale legislation.

On 20 August, 1998 Terry Cameron crossed the floor to support the second reading of the government's bill for the sale of ETSA. Having broken party rules binding all ALP members of parliament to support majority positions, he had no choice but to resign or be expelled. He chose to resign.

It still appeared that the government would not be able to get sufficient votes in the Legislative Council to support a trade sale. Facing the possibility that the sale would not proceed, the government re-visited the option of leasing the assets. This option had been rejected earlier by the Premier. He argued that it would result in a discount of around 20% on the sale proceeds. However, the Premier changed his view after an overseas trip to promote the sale of assets. He now claimed that he had advice that the proceeds from a lease would not be significantly less than a trade sale. 'It would be fair to say', asserted the Premier, 'given the advice we had earlier this year, that [the lease discount] might be in the 20 to 25% category, this is not the case, and every one of the potential investors I spoke to indicated that to me'. This shift to consideration of a lease rather than a trade sale of electricity assets appeared to be an attempt by the government to achieve privatisation via different means.

Facing possible defeat, the government intensified its sale campaign by warning that it would be forced to consider increases in state taxes and budget cuts if the sale did not proceed. The Treasurer, Rob Lucas argued that there was increased pressure on the State Budget arising from the risk that interest rates may rise, resulting in an increase in state debt repayments.

It became increasingly clear that Nick Xenophon was not going to support the government unless it agreed to reforms to the generation sector of the electricity industry in South Australia. Xenophon was critical of the government for choosing to support the construction of a new power station at Pelican Point rather than the establishment of an interconnector between South Australia and New South Wales. He argued the latter would have assisted in increasing competition in the South Australian electricity market and ensure greater security of supply. The government appeared reluctant to support the interconnector because of concerns that the link might reduce the value of South Australian generators.

On 26 October Nick Xenophon indicated that his support for a lease would be conditional on the government holding a referendum on the issue. The state government rejected the suggestion of a referendum. A long-term lease option was opposed by the Labor Opposition, Australian Democrats and No Pokies MP, Nick Xenophon. Nick Xenophon indicated that he would support a short-term lease of up to 25 years. He regarded a longer-term lease as 'a de facto sale'.

On 5 November 1998, the *Advertiser* launched an extraordinary attack on proponents of a lease suggesting that the government should ignore the will of parliament and proceed with a trade sale.

By accepting a lease the Parliament . . . would be . . . capitulating, quite literally selling out the interests of the electorate. . . . These two MPs [Nick Xenophon and Terry Cameron] should vote for the sale as, indeed, should the Labor Party and the Australian Democrats. If they will not do so, the Olsen government should force the issue. Take Parliament to the wire. The government should govern which, in this case, means sign a contract for the sale and be done with it. Do not put a sale contract on the table in Parliament: slam it down with great force.

The prospect of support for a lease from Nick Xenophon evaporated on 8 December 1998 when he declared that he had 'lost faith' in the government. He rejected the lease arguing that the state government would get more from supporting the establishment of the Riverlink interconnector with NSW than it would get from the sale of ETSA. The Premier strongly criticised Nick Xenophon's decision, indicating that the government would consider 'cuts to essential services, increases in taxes and charges or running the Budget at a deficit'.

The decision by Nick Xenophon created one major rupture in the otherwise solid business support base provided to the government. A key business figure, Ian Webber, director of the mining

companies Western Mining Corporation (WMC) and Santos indicated that he 'reluctantly' supported Xenophon's decision and that
there were 'reasons for concern' and 'issues that need to be addressed
in much greater depth'. Access to cheaper power may have been
uppermost in his mind as comments the following day from his
colleague, WMC executive Terry Dwyer indicated. Dwyer said that
WMC was considering building its own power station or purchasing
power from Victoria.

The government's attempts to bolster support for the sale were
once again supported by the *Advertiser* (29 January 1998) which ran
an editorial stating its 'support of energy asset sales out of sheer
budgetary necessity'.

In a further attempt to win support for the sale the government
backed away from its earlier commitment to use all of the proceeds
from the sale to pay off debt. On 28 January 1998 the Premier
announced that the government would establish a $1 billion ETSA
Reinvestment Fund using part of the proceeds of a sale or lease of
ETSA to fund new projects. These projects were to be in politically
sensitive areas such as job creation, education, the environment and
hospitals. This strategy had the potential to backfire given the
government's claim that debt reduction was central to its privatisation strategy. This shift appeared to be designed to win the support
of Trevor Crothers who had yet to declare his position.

Ironically, in an attempt to build support for the sale within the
Legislative Council, the government risked losing support in the
House of Assembly. Under these circumstances the ETSA
Reinvestment Fund was not a viable strategy. Realising this, the
government shifted its focus back to the risks it believed were associated with retaining ETSA under public ownership. Premier Olsen
suggested that the market was about to be flooded with the sale of
NSW electricity assets after the NSW state election, significantly
reducing the proceeds from the sale of ETSA.

However, by the end of 1998 it appeared that there was no
immediate prospect for the privatisation of the industry in NSW
unless the NSW Labor Party were defeated at the March 1999 state
election. Recognising that he would not get the support of the NSW
Labor Party for privatisation, Labor Premier Bob Carr was set to go

to the election opposing privatisation (*Daily Telegraph*, 10 October 1998, p. 4).

At the beginning of March Western Mining Corporation announced that the company had signed a contract for electricity with Yallourn Energy in Victoria. The Treasurer, Rob Lucas seized on this, arguing that it was an example of the risks associated with the emerging NEM and that ETSA was set to lose further major contracts in the new market. He argued that the loss of the WMC contract to ETSA was 'proof that ETSA could not compete against private sector operators'.

In an attempt to further increase pressure on those opposing the sale, the Treasurer announced on 2 March 1999 that all households in South Australia would have to pay an additional $186 electricity levy per annum as a consequence of the ETSA sale not proceeding. The 'Rann power bill' as he described it was 'solely the responsibility of those who oppose the sale'.

A poll of 500 voters undertaken by the *Advertiser* in February 1999 indicated that the government's primary vote had fallen from 41% to 37% over the month to February. However, while public opposition to the sale was high, this was not reflected in the coverage of the *Advertiser* newspaper which regularly featured comments from prominent business people and other figures supportive of the sale. These comments usually warned of an impending fiscal crisis if ETSA were not sold. The claims were usually highly rhetorical and rarely supported by any factual evidence. Former Premier of South Australia Steele Hall argued that the sale was essential because of a need to reduce state public debt. Hall supported the government's claims about the potential impact of the sale of NSW electricity assets on South Australia's relative competitive position. The head of the Real Estate Institute of SA, Trevor Dunsford suggested, without any evidence, that the failure to sell ETSA was slowing down house sales and went on to describe the ETSA debate as 'an emotional squabble between a pack of ferals who have lost sight of the ball'. His comments are illustrative of a wider sense of frustration expressed by business representatives and large companies supporting the sale. Other comments showed a willingness to intensify the pressure on the opponents of the sale. A group of South Australia's most prominent business people sponsored a full-page advertisement calling on the Labor Party, the Democrats and Nick Xenophon to support the sale. Without any substantiation of their claims they warned that: 'Taxes will rise. Business will leave. Jobs will go' if the sale did not go ahead.

The result of the NSW state election in March 1999 undermined the Olsen Government's arguments about the impact of the sale of NSW electricity assets on the value of South Australia's. After going to the NSW state election with a policy opposing privatisation of the electricity industry, the Carr Labor Government won convincingly. Widespread opposition to privatisation within the NSW community was regarded as a factor contributing to the re-election of Labor in NSW.

Having reached an impasse and with no clear sign that it would win the support it needed to pass the sale legislation in the upper house, the government was forced to disband the ETSA sale consultancy team. Around 40 consultants were working on the sale at the time. Over the 12 months to 24 April 1999 the government had spent around $30 million on the consultants.

In an effort to increase pressure on sale opponents, the government followed through with its threat to introduce a new ETSA tax on households if the sale did not go ahead. The May 1999 State Budget included an ETSA surcharge projecting an average increase of around $186 on household electricity bills. The Treasurer, Rob Lucas justified it, arguing that: 'The Parliament was given a clear choice of either supporting the sale or lease of ETSA and Optima and the associated ongoing financial benefits or, if it opposed ... a sale or lease, it would have to accept the alternative tax increases or expenditure reductions'.

Soon after the State Budget, it appeared that the government might be given the lifeline it needed to get the sale legislation through parliament. On 1 June 1999 Trevor Crothers shocked his Labor caucus colleagues by announcing that he was considering supporting a lease of ETSA if the state government met a number of conditions. He sought assurances from the government that the legislation would include guarantees for ETSA employees, including a choice of either 'relocation to another government job or a voluntary separation package of eight weeks plus three weeks for every year or service to a maximum of 104 weeks'. He also demanded that all of the proceeds from the lease be used to retire public debt. These relatively modest conditions were not likely to be rejected by the government.

On the following day Crothers outlined some of the reasons why he was considering supporting the government's proposal to lease ETSA. He echoed arguments put forward by the government, including the necessity for a reduction in public debt and for an improvement in South Australia's credit rating. With a reduction in public debt, he suggested that South Australia would become a more attractive investment proposition. Furthermore, the government would be in a better position to offer a financial inducement to firms like Mitsubishi to keep them in South Australia. Finally, he argued that the value of the assets would decline dramatically because the NSW Government was likely to sell its electricity assets soon, commenting: 'If that happens there will be nothing left in the kitty for SA to get a fair price for our assets'. These arguments indicated that Crothers appeared to be on the verge of giving his support to the government. Later that day he met with the Treasurer, Rob Lucas to discuss the conditions he sought in order to provide support for the lease.

Recognising that Trevor Crothers was likely to support the privatisation of ETSA, the Leader of the Opposition, Mike Rann, sought to dissuade him, arguing that privatisation of the electricity industry would result in higher electricity prices and the loss of 'control . . . of ETSA to foreign investors who have no interest in the welfare of . . . the community or in the development of the South Australian economy'.

After written reassurances from the government, Trevor Crothers crossed the floor in the upper house to support a 'test clause' in the government's sale legislation on 3 June 1999. This paved the way for the government to pass the legislation in full. In the end it appears that, while Crothers was not prepared to agree to the sale of ETSA, he was willing to support a lease of the assets even though this was for all practical purposes equivalent to a sale. Crothers later provided an insight into his change of mind. He revealed that he had met with the Premier:

Six to eight weeks before the 3 June vote and Olsen [the Premier] asked me to come down to his office. He said to me, 'Would you consider changing your mind over the sale of ETSA?' 'Save your breath. The short and the long of it is I will not support the sale of ETSA.' . . . As I got up to leave, as a throwaway line Olsen said: 'Would you consider leasing ETSA?' I paused, then I went back and sat down again. It was my duty as elected member to support the lease to get the state back into the black. Anything less would have been a dereliction of my duty.

There is considerable inconsistency in the arguments put forward by Crothers. His close ties with Terry Cameron as a member of the 'once dominant' centre-left faction of the ALP, the ostracism faced by Cameron before and after his decision to support the sale, and Crothers' own growing alienation within the ALP, appear to have contributed to his change of mind.

The defections of Cameron and Crothers reflect the breakdown of factional and ideological ties within the ALP which failed in the end to bind them to the majority party decision. It appears that, despite Labor's strong public opposition to the sale of ETSA, a number of Labor MPs privately supported privatisation. In an attempt to fuel division over the sale of ETSA within the ALP, the Treasurer, Rob Lucas suggested that eight members of the Labor caucus had indicated to him that they supported the sale.

That Cameron and Crothers were prepared to support the sale might reflect growing ambivalence within the ALP about the role of government in the provision of goods and services. In the end, however, the decision of these two to support privatisation may have had more to do with thwarted ambitions and growing alienation within the ALP rather than with the relative merits of public versus private ownership of the electricity industry. Indeed one commentator suggested that privatisation could have been prevented if Labor members had spent more time persuading Crothers to oppose the sale.

The lease goes ahead
The legislation enabling the lease of ETSA was passed in the lower house of State Parliament on 10 June 1999. While Labor voted

against the lease, they enabled the government to extend the duration of the lease from 25 to 99 years. This was not universally supported by Labor MPs, with a small number arguing that Labor should not have supported any element of the government's legislation.

As soon as the legislation was passed, the team of consultants working on the privatisation of ETSA were 're-activated' and electricity privatisation brokers around the world were informed. A month later the Treasurer, Rob Lucas, announced that he would visit the US to talk with a range of companies about the privatisation process.

With the legislation cleared through parliament, the government acted quickly to get the privatisation process underway. It established an indicative timetable for disposal of the generation assets. This aimed to achieve financial close on the disposal of the assets by the middle of 2000.

On 2 August 1999 the government announced that it had leased Flinders Power to a US-based firm, NRG Energy. The 100-year lease, valued at around $465 million, involved a number of generation assets, including the Northern and Playford coal-fired power stations at Port Augusta, the Leigh Creek coal mine, a rail line linking the mine and the power stations and the 'company' township of Leigh Creek. The lease also included responsibility for the management of the long-term power purchase contract for the Osborne generator.

On 12 December 1999 the government leased ETSA Utilities, ETSA's electricity distribution network, for 200 years to Hong Kong-based Hutchson Whampoa group for $3.5 billion. The group made its bid for ETSA Utilities through a joint venture involving Hong Kong Electric and Cheung Kong Infrastructure (CKI). Prior to securing the deal CKI already had a presence in South Australia, as an investor in Envestra, an energy firm operating Adelaide's gas network.

There was an immediate challenge to the outcome of the bidding process by Utilicorp, a US-based bidder for the lease. A spokesperson stated that they were 'absolutely stunned' that CKI won the bid and claimed that their bid 'was worth more than $100 million more than the CKI bid'. Utilicorp questioned the outcome, complaining that: 'They've awarded the bid to a party for $100 million less and that party had no expertise in South Australia. I would have thought they wanted to get Australian ownership, with expertise in Australia'. Treasurer Rob Lucas, however, championed the outcome as 'the best lease that's ever been recorded'. He claimed that it 'was in the top 10 out of 73 power sales or lease agreements in Australia, the United Kingdom and US during the past five years'. Finally he argued that the deal maximised 'debt retirement and minimise[d] risk to taxpayers'. However, these claims did not go unchallenged.

While criticism of the outcome by Utilicorp raised some questions about the integrity of the bidding process, the government was soon able to deflect attention away from this issue and focus on the reaction to the lease decision by the credit rating agency, Standard and Poors. On 15 December 1999 Standard and Poors announced that they would upgrade South Australia's credit rating from AA to AA+. Despite earlier claims of the importance to the government of a credit rating upgrade, the Treasurer, Rob Lucas indicated that the upgrade would not have a significant impact on South Australians after all, commenting that: 'The biggest impact is in terms of the public and business perception and state morale. It's also about how everyone looks at us in terms of investment – do they look at us and think we are a bit of basket case? The second area's in terms of borrowing costs and our advice is that it can have a small impact but we are not overstating that . . .'. The real financial and economic benefits of a credit upgrade are relatively insignificant. The South Australian Commission of Audit (1994, p. 18) estimated that an upgrade from AA to AA+ would be less than $1 million per annum.

Any potential financial benefits of a credit rating upgrade fade into insignificance when compared to the costs of consultants engaged to drive the ETSA sale process. The Auditor General confirmed that total payments made to consultants over the 1997–98 to 2000–01 period reached $114 million. Included in these were payments of $56 million for legal advice, $25 million to the lead advisors and $18 million for accounting advice (Auditor General 2001, p. 895).

Reflections on the debate

As early as 1995, the state government was secretly considering the privatisation of ETSA and it was involved in investigating options for this process before and immediately after the 1997 state election. Despite these activities, the government went to the election pledging it would not privatise ETSA. It argued that retaining ETSA was financially beneficial to the state and that it made no sense to sell a profitable public enterprise which returned significant dividends to the State Budget. The retention of ETSA in public ownership accorded with widespread opposition to privatisation within the South Australian community, a view reflected in other states, including New South Wales and Tasmania where opposition to the sale of the electricity industry had prevailed. Soon after re-election the South Australian Liberal Government claimed that it had new information that demonstrated that it was too risky to retain public ownership of ETSA and that it was necessary to privatise the industry to eliminate these risks.

The government derived its initial justification for the sale of ETSA by claiming that it was presented with new information when both ETSA's annual report and the Auditor General's annual report were tabled in State Parliament in December 1997. The government argued initially that the $97 million write-down of ETSA outlined in the 1997 ETSA annual report demonstrated that ETSA was not able to effectively manage the risks associated with participation in the emerging competitive electricity market. The government pleaded ignorance of the write-down, although all the evidence, as we have seen, points to the government being aware of the write-down well before the release of the annual report. The $97 million write-down presented no threat to ETSA's viability and was disclosed as a manageable matter.

Utilising advice provided by consultants and the former Auditor General, Tom Sheridan, the government argued that sale prices between $4–5 billion would result in net financial gains to the State Budget. Alternative analyses suggested otherwise. In particular Quiggin and Spoehr (1998) argued that sale prices in excess of $7 billion were necessary before any net benefit was likely to be derived. Despite the 1997 state election campaign claim that South Australia's financial position was sound, the government, after winning the election, argued that the state faced bankruptcy unless ETSA were sold. Furthermore, accelerated debt reduction was held to be imperative even though public debt levels were projected to reach historically low levels without further assets sales. The benefits of a credit rating upgrade as a consequence of a sale were proclaimed, yet an upgrade was likely to result in only a small reduction in public debt interest repayments. There is no legitimate basis in this context for the government's argument that public services would have to be cut and taxes increased if ETSA were not sold.

In the end the Liberal Government's arguments for the privatisation of ETSA were hollow and opportunistic. It is clear that the state government was committed to the privatisation of ETSA well before the 1997 state election. The policy backflip in 1998 was not based on sound reasoning and the need to adapt to changing circumstances, but rather on political opportunism in the pursuit of an ideological commitment to privatisation. In its first two years of office it had undertaken extensive privatisations in the areas of information technology, public transport, health and water. There is little doubt that the government would have lost the 1997 state election had it announced its intention to privatise ETSA prior to the election. To achieve its objective and survive electorally, it was necessary to wait until just after the 1997 state election before embarking upon a second wave of privatisations. It is likely that the government anticipated that public dissatisfaction with the ETSA privatisation would dissipate before it went to the polls in 2002. The result of that election suggests otherwise.

Given the prominence of concerns about electricity pricing issues throughout 2001 and the prospect of power blackouts during the 2002 state election, there was a strong chance that electricity issues would be high in the agenda during the election campaign. As it turned out, South Australia had one of the coolest beginnings to summer in recorded history. Despite this, privatisation was a key concern of the election campaign with the ALP focussing on it in all their early publicity. The result of the election suggests that dissatisfaction with privatisation had eroded support for the Liberal Government but Labor just fell short of getting the majority it needed to form government in its own right.

On 4 March 2002 the ALP won a no-confidence vote on the floor of State Parliament, enabling it to form government with the support of Peter Lewis, the Member for Hammond. History seems to repeat itself in strange and ironic ways. One Liberal vote enabled the nationalisation of the electricity industry in 1946. One Labor vote enabled the privatisation of ETSA in 1998. One ex-Liberal member enabled Labor to form government in 2002. The ironies of this will not be lost on close observers of history.

References

Advertiser, various issues, 1997–2000.

Auditor General 2001, *Annual Report*, Adelaide.

Australian, various issues, 1997–1999.

Electricity Sector Reform Unit 1996, 'To the Electricity Reform Cabinet Committee. Adelaide', Government of South Australia.

Evans, S 1998, 'Democrats zap SA power sell-off', *Financial Review*, 26 June, p. 5.

Janes, M 1998a, 'Electricity reform in South Australia', Adelaide, South Australia, Parliament of South Australia, Economic and Finance Committee.

____1998b, 'Letter to Hon Dr Michael Armitage MBBS, MP', ETSA Corporation.

Quiggin, J & Spoehr, J 1998, 'The proposed privatisation of the South Australian electricity industry: An economic analysis', United Trades and Labour Council of South Australia, Adelaide.

Sheridan, T 1998, 'An assessment of issues pertaining to the sale of ETSA and Optima', Adelaide.

South Australia, Commission of Audit 1993, *Report*, Adelaide.

South Australia, House of Assembly 1998, Debates, 1994–1999, Adelaide.

CHAPTER 4

Free Market Reform and the South Australian Electricity Supply Industry

JOHN QUIGGIN

Introduction

The electricity industry has undergone radical market-oriented reforms in Australia. From the Second World War until the early 1980s, electricity in Australia was provided by public monopolies owned primarily by state governments, and operated as statutory authorities. Although the arrangements differed in their details, the electricity industry in each state was characterised by a high degree of vertical and horizontal integration and a substantial degree of autonomy.

The Electricity Trust of South Australia (ETSA) was a typical example. Like electricity authorities in other states, ETSA was controlled primarily by engineers and pursued objectives defined in terms of meeting the needs of households and business for a reliable supply of electricity, with prices being set to cover average costs.

The reforms of the 1980s and 1990s – many of which resulted in privatisation – were designed to change almost every aspect of the pre-reform institutional framework. It was hoped that the integrated, state-owned and bureaucratically run electricity monopolies would be replaced by a profit-oriented, privately owned industry, operating in a competitive national market characterised by a clear separation between the activities of generation, transmission and distribution, and retailing. Consumers would be able to choose their supplier in a competitive retail market.

Much of this policy agenda has now been implemented. The implementation of the National Electricity Market (NEM) is approaching its final stage, that of full retail contestability (FRC) – although full retail contestability has been rejected in Queensland.

The privatisation component of the research agenda has been successful although voters in New South Wales rejected privatisation, as did the ACT Legislative Assembly. In South Australia however, the Olsen Government privatised the electricity industry after inducing two members of the Upper House, elected as ALP candidates, to cross the floor. The main generation and distribution components of ETSA were leased in 1999 and 2000.

In this chapter the experience of market-oriented reform and privatisation is assessed and the desirability of a move towards full retail contestability is discussed.

International experience

Advocates of privatisation and competitive deregulation of electricity markets have relied heavily on the existence of an international trend in favour of these policies. However, recent developments have undermined many of these arguments.

Competitive electricity markets, broadly similar to the Australian National Electricity Market (NEM), have been established in a number of countries. Assessments of the resulting outcomes have varied. The two most important cases are that of the United Kingdom, regarded by most observers as a partial success, and that of California, which was an unequivocal failure.

The UK system allowed for electricity to be sold both through long-term contracts and through a spot market or 'pool'. Although most evaluations of the electricity reforms in the United Kingdom have been, on balance, positive, serious problems emerged. To maintain high sale prices, the generating component of the former public monopoly was divided into only two main firms. In combination with design features of the pool, this gave rise to opportunities for the two main suppliers to extract monopoly rent through strategic bidding (Green & Newbery 1992). In 1998, the pool was abolished. Opinion remains divided as to whether this decision was an appropriate response, or whether design changes

to the pool could have yielded superior outcomes, as argued by
Newbery (1997).

The Californian market, like that in Australia, was established at
a time of excess supply of electricity, and took the opposite approach
to that embodied in the 1998 reforms in the United Kingdom.
Long-term contracts were prohibited and all sales were required to go
through the spot market. Moreover, retail prices for most consumers
remained fixed.

Problems with the Californian system did not become evident
until the (northern) summer of 2000, when the system was barely
able to meet peak demands. By the end of 2000, the market price of
electricity had risen from $50/MWh to $500/MWh. The main distributors, Pacific Gas and Electric and Southern California Edison,
who were required to buy electricity at market prices and sell it at
fixed retail prices, faced bankruptcy. On 8 January 2001, the state
governor announced that the deregulation scheme, which he called
a 'colossal and dangerous failure', would be abandoned.

Supporters of the Australian electricity reforms have generally
sought to play down the difficulties experienced in the United
Kingdom and to argue that the failure of the Californian system was
due to incomplete deregulation and, in particular, the cap on retail
prices and the prohibition of long-term contracts. The latter claim
has some validity, but is subject to important qualifications.

As will be argued below, any system of electricity markets faces
a tension between the short-term function of electricity prices in allo-
cating a scarce and non-storable resource and the long-term function
of providing appropriate investment signals. Neither in the United
Kingdom nor in California have these roles been properly reconciled.
In addition, many Australian advocates of electricity reform have
relied on short-term experience of declining prices to argue that the
reforms have been beneficial. As the Californian experience shows, an
excessive focus on reducing prices in periods of excess supply can
contribute to system failure in periods of excess demand.

Also relevant in this context are the numerous allegations of
collusive or otherwise monopolistic behaviour by market participants which characterised the Californian crisis. There is no reason
to suppose that similar market manipulation is not feasible in

Australia. Ironically, domestic criticism of the Californian arrangements was led by the Enron Corporation, the leading participant in, and most prominent advocate of, the deregulated energy trading system. Enron itself has now collapsed, primarily as a result of large losses from related-party transactions, casting doubt on its claims that existing regulations were unduly restrictive. Implications for Enron's Australian energy trading operations remain unclear.

Finally, it is always possible, *ex post*, to explain the failure of a system in terms of inappropriate implementation. A crucial feature of system design is that systems should be robust to minor errors and unexpected shocks. Repeated failures, no matter how easily explicable in retrospect, are evidence that the system as a whole is flawed. It is necessary to consider the extent to which the Australian system has the robustness required for a system in which even brief failures are extremely costly.

The National Grid and the National Electricity Market

This section describes the process leading up to the creation of the National Grid and the National Electricity Market.

The National Grid

As was economically rational in the light of Australia's geography, separate electricity supply industries were initially established in each state. Limited connections between Victoria and New South Wales were established as part of the Snowy Mountains Hydro-electric Scheme, which also created a new generator, the Snowy Mountains Hydro-electric Corporation. A link between Victoria and South Australia was added subsequently.

In physical terms, plans for the National Grid involved the expansion of existing interstate links and the creation of a range of new links, including Riverlink which connects New South Wales and South Australia. The plans for the National Grid also allowed scope for private initiatives to enable the construction of additional links. In practice, most of the additional links ran into political and environmental difficulties. In particular, the construction of Riverlink was rejected by the South Australian Government when it appeared that it was likely to reduce the sale price that could be realised in the privatisation of ETSA. The creation of a fully operational national grid is still some years away.

The creation of a national grid is a necessary condition for the creation of a national market, but it does not necessarily imply the creation of such a market. In a different policy environment, the decision to build a national grid could have been the precursor to the establishment of a unified national electricity supplier comparable to Telecom Australia. More realistically, the existing arrangements for trade between the states could have formed the basis for the more frequent and extensive trading made possible by the National Grid.

The National Electricity Market

Following the agreement to construct a national grid in 1991, attention turned to the design of the National Electricity Market, modelled primarily on that of the United Kingdom. Although it was already evident that the British model had serious flaws, it was hoped that Australia could learn from the British experience.

The core of the market was the creation of a continuous-time auction market, in which generators and users enter bids on a half-hourly basis. Each bid takes the form of a supply or demand schedule which identifies a willingness to supply or demand electricity. These bids are combined to form aggregate demand-and-supply schedules.

Because available capacity and consumption can fluctuate, 'market clearing' is undertaken at five-minute intervals. The intersection of the aggregate demand-and-supply schedules determines the dispatch price required to equate demand and supply for the given five-minute period. All generators with bids less than or equal to the dispatch price have their bids accepted, and, conversely, all users with bids greater than or equal to the dispatch price have their demand met. These prices are averaged over a half-hour period to determine a spot price, which is the price received by generators and paid by purchasers. In addition to spot purchases, participants in the market may enter into long-term bilateral contracts or trade in a forward market. The Australian spot and forward markets are operated by a private limited-liability company – the National Electricity Market Management Company (NEMMCO).

Disaggregation

Before the reforms, the electricity industry in South Australia, as in other states, displayed a high degree of vertical and horizontal integration. ETSA was an integrated monopoly which provided all electricity services, from generation, transmission and distribution to metering and billing, and even mined some of the coal used for generation.

A crucial element of the reforms was the vertical and horizontal disintegration of the industry. Vertical disintegration was undertaken by separating the industry into the separate components of generation, transmission, distribution and retailing. Each of these components was horizontally disaggregated into separate firms to encourage competition.

An aggressive approach to horizontal disaggregation was consistent with the policy atmosphere of the early 1990s, which saw, for example, the construction of parallel optical fibre telecommunications networks in several Australian cities. It was also encouraged by a critical evaluation of the British electricity market. Green and Newbery (1992) examined the British market design and concluded that the market structure would allow for the extraction of substantial monopoly rents.

The designers of the Australian National Electricity Market sought to avoid the anticompetitive features of the British market, and therefore encouraged the break-up of state electricity generation enterprises on horizontal as well as vertical lines. As part of this process, ETSA was broken into separate enterprises providing generation (Flinders, Optima and Synergen), transmission (ElectraNet), distribution (ETSA Utilities) and retail (ETSA) services.

The restructuring of the electricity industry was based on the presumption that economies of scale and scope are relatively unimportant. The vertical separation of generation, transmission and distribution eliminates any economies of scope that might have arisen with an integrated supplier. Moreover, the creation of a number of small generators implies the loss of economies of scale that might be achieved by larger firms. An alternative interpretation of the restructuring process is that the break-up of state electricity monopolies is a prelude to re-integration of the industry achieved through mergers between companies operating in different states, most of which, in turn, would be subsidiaries of multinational electricity enterprises.

Retail contestability

Initially electricity consumers were supplied by the existing distribution enterprises at prices fixed by regulation. The final stage of implementation of the NEM involved a gradual shift to retail 'contestability' in which consumers would be able to choose a retailer for their electricity. The retailer would be responsible for purchasing wholesale electricity, paying the distributor for the use of the network and for services such as billing and metering. Distributors were allowed to continue to provide retail services, but were required to undertake elaborate 'ring-fencing' exercises to ensure that their retail services did not obtain unfair advantages as a result of joint ownership.

In the first instance retail contestability was applied for large and medium-sized consumers only. Because the NEM was introduced at a time of excess supply, prices in the wholesale electricity market were well below their long-run average level. These price reductions were passed on to contestable customers, while retail consumers continued to pay fixed prices set roughly equal to long-run average cost. It was widely suggested that, when full retail contestability was introduced, ordinary consumers would enjoy the benefits of competition, previously confined to large businesses.

In reality, the period of excess supply was short-lived. Even before the introduction of full retail contestability, wholesale prices had risen and there was considerable pressure to pass these increases on to households as well as to contestable customers.

The separation of retailing and distribution is based partly on the belief that consumers will benefit from a choice between competing packages of electricity pricing and billing, and partly out of concern to limit, as far as possible, the natural monopoly component of the industry. However, for most households, and particularly in the absence of sophisticated metering, electricity is a fairly simple commodity. Assuming prices are set at an appropriate level, it may be that most householders will prefer to continue buying their electricity from the distributor as they have done in the past. The problem is that this option may not be available, or may entail a substantial increase in prices, as has occurred in Victoria.

The organisation of the National Electricity Market and the retail electricity market also implied the creation of a wholesaling function in electricity. Electricity is purchased in five-minute blocks in the market, but retail consumers expect constant prices over periods of a month or a quarter. It is necessary therefore that some market participants should undertake the function of buying electricity at the spot price and supplying it in wholesale quantities at a stable wholesale price. This function is conceptually distinct from the retail activity of providing metering and billing services in return for a mark-up on the wholesale price. In much discussion of the electricity market it seems to be assumed that wholesaling will be integrated with retailing. However, as is argued below, the wholesaling function must be primarily concerned with risk management, while the retailing function is concerned with customer service. It seems unlikely that joint provision of wholesale and retail services will yield positive economies of scope.

In summary, it seems unlikely at this stage that retail contestability will work as anticipated by its advocates. Most consumers will have few options but to remain with their existing distributors, but the protection provided under the statutory monopoly system will gradually be eroded.

Theoretical issues in electricity markets
Competition and prices

Much discussion of electricity reform in Australia is based on the assumption that 'competition reduces prices'. Hence, the decline in the cost of electricity, at least for contestable users, which occurred in the aftermath of the introduction of the National Electricity Market, was seen as evidence that the reforms were working well. It was predicted that, with the advent of full retail contestability, similar benefits would flow to household users of electricity.

Such an interpretation was simplistic and failed to take account of the way in which the electricity pool and spot market operated. In the short term, any reduction in costs resulting from competitive long-run average pricing will generally be small in relation to the greater variability in prices associated with the operation of the spot market. The dominant effect of the introduction of a competitive spot market will be to push prices below long-run average cost in periods of excess capacity and to raise prices above long-run average cost in periods of excess demand. This variation in prices is crucial if the electricity market is to perform efficiently and provide appropriate investment signals.

Planning and prices

Before the introduction of the National Electricity Market, the electricity supply industry operated on the basis of central planning. New generating capacity was constructed on the basis of estimates of future 'needs', sometimes subject to constraints on the availability of capital. Short-run operation of the system relied on the concept of an 'order of merit' that determined which units of generating capacity would be used to supply demand. Broadly speaking, low-cost 'base-load' stations were designed to operate continuously, supplemented by higher-cost peakload capacity in periods of higher demand.

In an electricity market, the central planner is replaced by price signals. In the short run, generators submit bids specifying their willingness to supply electricity at particular prices. These bids are matched with demand from purchasers of electricity to determine the spot price. The spot price not only balances the market in the short term, but also provides firms with information on the likely profitability of investments in new generating capacity .

Weaknesses of the price mechanism

The crucial feature that distinguishes the spot electricity market from most other markets for goods and services is the variability of prices. Even in the most variable commodity markets, it is rare for prices to vary by more than a factor of ten in the course of a single year. By contrast, in the National Electricity Market prices routinely vary by a factor of 500 from one day to the next. While prices in periods of excess capacity usually vary between $20/MWh and $40/MWh, the price in periods of excess demand frequently reaches the maximum of $10,000/MWh. Although periods of excess demand are rare, they account for a significant proportion of the annual revenue accruing to generators. For example, if the price is normally $20/MWh, but reaches the peak price of $10,000/MWh for four hours during each of four days per year, these four days will account for approximately half of the annual revenue accruing to generators.

A number of difficulties arise here. First, there is the regulatory limit of $10,000/MWh. The theory underlying the spot market is based on the absence of any such regulatory constraints. There is no clear justification for the choice of an upper limit of $10,000 as opposed to say $5000 or $20,000, yet these alternative choices lead to large differences in the annual revenue accruing to generators. This in turn implies that investment signals will be significantly distorted by the choice of an inappropriate upper limit.

A second set of difficulties, at least in the short term, arises from the fact that most final consumers (that is, householders) are not connected to meters sufficiently sophisticated to respond to price variations (or even, in many cases, time-of-day variations). Hence, the demand side of the price-signalling mechanism is ineffective. Moreover, the mismatch between highly variable producer prices and fixed consumer prices requires wholesalers to absorb variation in their margins or to seek insurance against price variations.

The third problem arises when suppliers possess market power. Because short-run demand is highly inelastic, even modest market power can yield large monopoly rents. These issues, and the effectiveness of competitive restructuring as a response, are discussed below.

Finally, and most importantly in this context, price variation can create serious problems in the absence of adequate mechanisms for managing risk. As will be argued in the following section, the capacity of the NEM institutions to deal appropriately with risk remains in doubt.

Risk

Risk is a crucial, but often neglected, issue in the operation of the NEM. Even where risk has been discussed, advocates of the NEM have frequently misunderstood the key issues, particularly in relation to the role of the public sector.

In the period of public provision, most risk was internalised by integrated electricity supply enterprises. Variations in demand were dealt with through the maintenance of a degree of excess capacity, allowing the operating of an 'order-of-merit' allocation system. Under this system, demand was met first by low-cost 'baseload' power stations. As demand rose, higher-cost generating stations were brought into operation. Peaks in demand were met, in part through interruptible supply agreements, under which some large business users received lower rates in return for allowing the electricity suppliers to cut their supplies in peak periods.

The only risk borne directly by consumers was the risk of supply interruption arising either from a breakdown in some part of the system or from (very rare) cases when supply was inadequate to meet demand. As owners of electricity supply enterprises, governments bore the risk associated with fluctuations in the demand for electricity, but given the relative stability of total demand and the integrated nature of the system, this risk was relatively small.

Output price risk was essentially non-existent. Not only were prices stable, but public ownership implied that any loss to government from setting prices too low was matched by a benefit to consumers. Conversely, any increase in profits from setting prices too high was offset by a loss to consumers.

Governments bore risks relating to costs. However, these risks were relatively modest, due to the technologically mature and capital-intensive nature of the industry.

The main cost associated with the approach to risk management adopted under the public system was the need to maintain a relatively high level of excess capacity. This was associated with a willingness to accept higher employment levels than were technically required, although, as will be argued below, a number of factors contributed to the relatively high labour costs of the public system.

Critics of the public system focussed on the costs of excess capacity and generally ignored problems of risk management. As a result, the design of the NEM and the associated reforms to the electricity industry exacerbated existing risks and introduced new ones.

The reduction in excess capacity and in the employment of maintenance staff increased the relatively small risk of a prolonged and complete system failure. No such failure has yet been experienced in the Australian electricity industry, but there have been a series of failures in infrastructure industries that have followed a similar reform path. These include the Adelaide 'Big Pong' arising from the failure of the sewage filtration system and the disruption of gas supplies to Melbourne following the fatal explosion at Esso's Longford plant.

The reform process, including privatisation, disaggregation and the operations of the NEM create a complex range of price risks, most of which did not exist under the public system. Most obviously, the fluctuations in prices inherent in the system create risks for generators and, in the absence of price equalisation, for consumers. The design of the market is based on the assumption that consumers will be able to dissipate risk through contracts with retailers and wholesalers.

A separate set of risks apply to transmission and distribution. Returns on these activities are set by regulation. Under privatisation, the internalisation of medium-term price risk which characterised the public system is lost. If regulated rates of return are set too high, income is transferred from consumers to the (normally foreign) owners of transmission and distribution enterprises. If rates of return are set too low, income is transferred to consumers.

Political incentives obviously favour lower rates of return and, therefore, lower electricity prices. Hence, owners of distribution and transmission enterprises are likely to undertake extensive lobbying and will also seek to make as credible as possible the threat that, if rates of return are set too low, vitally needed investments will not be undertaken. Hence, investment decisions may be made in a strategic fashion, to enhance the firm's bargaining position when seeking to influence regulatory outcomes. Both individual firms and their representative body, the Electricity Supply Association of Australia, are engaged in lobbying. Evidence of strategic investment is harder to obtain, but as the system matures, strategic approaches are likely to be refined.

The costs of risk in the new system are difficult to assess, but undoubtedly substantial. Some components of the cost of risk can be quantified using observed prices in capital markets. However, the prospects for a market solution to risk problems have been clouded by the catastrophic collapse of Enron, the firm which created and dominated many of the relevant markets. Another set of costs relates to breakdowns in the complex trading arrangements for risk. Such breakdowns can involve expensive litigation and the dissipation of assets in bankruptcy proceedings.

More recently, Enron, the leading energy-trading enterprise in the United States, filed for bankruptcy as a result of related-party transactions and mis-statement of contingent risks. In view of the Californian crisis and the Enron collapse, it seems reasonable to conclude that the market for eliminating electricity risk in the United States has effectively failed.

Privatisation

Quiggin (1995) discusses characteristics that make an enterprise more or less suitable for privatisation. Small enterprises with modest capital requirements, operating in competitive markets with little need for regulation are most suitable for privatisations. Large capital-intensive enterprises operating in highly regulated markets with considerable monopoly power are least suitable.

In the context of the National Electricity Market, the break-up of integrated monopoly suppliers has produced enterprises with radically different characteristics. Electricity retailers and wholesalers appear very well suited for privatisation, except to the extent that distributors retain a retail function. On the other hand, transmission and distribution activities are natural monopolies requiring continuing regulation. Generation has intermediate characteristics, suggesting the possibility of a mixture of public and private operators.

In practice, however, distinctions of this kind have not been drawn in Australian policy debates. A major source of difficulty is the fact that transmission and distribution assets account for the majority of the capital value of the industry, while the market value of publicly owned retail assets is negligible. Hence, a proposal to privatise retail assets alone, or even retail and generation assets, has little appeal to governments concerned with the cosmetic effects of asset sales on budget balances and levels of public debt. Hence, privatisation proposals have normally involved the sale of the entire industry. On the other hand, politicians opposed to privatisation have generally found it easier to maintain a stance of unqualified support for the *status quo*.

Outcomes of electricity reform
Effect on consumers

As has been noted above, supporters of reforms to the electricity market made unfounded estimates of potential benefits based on the short-term decline in prices for contestable consumers which followed the introduction of the NEM. It would be equally inappropriate to base a critical assessment of the NEM on the price increases experienced in the past two years, some of which will probably prove temporary.

A complete assessment of the impact of electricity reform on consumers requires an estimate of the resulting change in average prices and in the variability of prices. No final judgement can be reached on these issues. Nevertheless, it seems reasonable to judge that household consumers of electricity will probably be worse off and that business consumers will, in general, be better off.

This is clearly true of the initial impact of reform. Business users became contestable in the early period of excess supply and were able to sign long-term contracts at low prices. Household users received none of the initial benefits and are now bearing the burden of price increases designed, in part, to recoup the earlier losses incurred by generators. Even if the differences in prices for households and businesses diminish in the future, there is no reason to suppose that these initial transfers will be reversed.

Even after the transitional phase is complete, it is likely that household consumers will be worse off. In many cases, the public system included cross-subsidies that benefitted households and these cross-subsidies have been removed in the new system. More importantly, in the absence of sophisticated metering and a capacity to manage household electricity use on an hourly basis in response to price movements, the variability of pool prices represents a pure cost to household consumers. Retailers and wholesalers are supposed to absorb this risk but will obviously charge a price premium for doing so.

The decision by the Queensland Government not to move to

full retail contestability reflects these considerations. In the government's public statement, the desire to maintain cross-subsidies between urban and rural consumers was emphasised. However, the difficulties of implementing a reasonable system of metering and billing in the context of fluctuating pool prices was also an important factor in the government's decision.

Effect on employment

Microeconomic reform has generally been associated with reductions in employment, and the electricity industry has been no exception. Between 1993 and 1997, the number of employees at ETSA fell from 4223 to 2544 and this decline has continued during the breakup and subsequent privatisation of ETSA.

The decline in employment may be attributed to a number of factors. First, the pre-reform electricity industry was characterised by a degree of 'feather-bedding'; that is, the number of employees was such that employees enjoyed a slower pace of work and more 'downtime' (time paid for but not actually engaged in productive activity) than other members of the Australian workforce. Not only has feather-bedding been eliminated, but the pace and intensity of work has increased in line with general trends in the Australian labour market. At least in periods of strong employment growth, reductions in 'feather-bedding' may yield net gains to society, since displaced workers can be re-employed in more productive activity. However, increases in work intensity have gone well beyond this point. In general, reductions in wages and increases in work intensity represent a transfer from workers to employers with no net benefit to society as a whole.

A second factor has been the replacement of direct employment by the use of external contractors. The use of competitive tendering and contracting may reduce costs in a variety of ways, but savings commonly arise from reductions in wages and working conditions.

A third factor in employment reductions in infrastructure service has been a reduction in the frequency and comprehensiveness of maintenance. Even though the inherent reliability of mature infrastructure technology has generally improved over recent decades, the period since the introduction of competitive reforms has seen a number of spectacular system failures, such as the Auckland blackout and the Longford gas explosion. Such failures may be attributed, at least in part, to declining maintenance standards.

The market and the environment

Electricity production gives rise to a number of environmental externalities of which the most important is the emission of carbon dioxide as a result of the combustion of carbon-based fossil fuels. Carbon dioxide is the most important of the 'greenhouse gases' which contribute to global warming. The most important issue not addressed in the design of the NEM is that of greenhouse gas emissions. In the current Australian electricity system, baseload electricity is usually generated by older coal-fired power stations, while newer stations, particularly those built to meet peak load requirements, are typically gas-fired and therefore give rise to smaller emissions of carbon dioxide for each unit of electricity generated. Both interconnections and the pool-pricing system of the NEM tend to encourage greater use of baseload coal-fired stations, which have lower fuel costs per unit of electricity, and therefore raise emissions of carbon dioxide.

The short-run impact of the National Electricity Market has been to reduce prices in periods of low demand to levels approximately equal to the market cost of the fuel consumed in generation. This reduction in prices has contributed to an increase in total greenhouse gas emissions from electricity generation, which rose from 129.1 million tonnes in 1990 to 168.6 million tonnes in 1998.

Since the market price of fuel does not incorporate any implicit or explicit externality charge, it is reasonable to conclude that the price of fuel (and therefore the price of electricity) is below the socially optimal level, and therefore that the operation of the National Electricity Market has contributed to excessive consumption of electricity and fossil fuels.

The adverse environmental effects of the National Electricity Market are likely to decrease in the long run, as excess capacity is reduced by the retirement of older coal-fired plants, and as carbon taxes or similar market-based policies to reduce emissions are introduced. However, as the economist Keynes appositely observed, in the long run we are all dead.

The design of the NEM is based on the assumption that, in the absence of an explicit regulatory response by governments, such as the imposition of a carbon tax, environmental impacts should be disregarded. Under the rules of the NEM code and Australian Competition and Consumer Commission (ACCC) requirements, the regulatory test defines market benefit as the total net benefits of the proposed augmentation to all those who produce, distribute and consume electricity in the National Electricity Market. Further, note 3 of the regulatory test states that the costs identified in determining the market benefit should include the cost of complying with existing and anticipated laws, regulations and administrative determinations, such as those dealing with health and safety, land management and environment pollution and the abatement of pollution. An environmental tax should be treated as part of a project's cost. An environmental subsidy should be treated as part of a project's benefits or as a negative cost. Any other costs should be disregarded.

The most direct response to the problem of greenhouse gas emissions would be the imposition of a 'carbon tax' set at a level which would be consistent with the satisfaction of Australia's obligations under the Kyoto protocol. This would raise the price of fuels with high carbon content and ensure that the price signals transmitted through the NEM reflect the costs of environmental damage.

Effects on citizens of the privatisation of ETSA

On 17 February 1998, the South Australian Government announced that it intended to privatise ETSA, the publicly owned operator of the state's electricity industry, thereby abandoning a commitment made during the 1997 election campaign. On 12 December 1999, the government announced the long-term lease of its distribution company, ETSA Utilities, and the sale of retail company ETSA Power for a total of $3.5 billion (later increased to $3.55 billion when ETSA was resold by the leaseholders). The remaining parts of the industry (the three generation companies Flinders, Optima and Synergen, and the transmission company ElectraNet) were leased or sold during 2000.

The Olsen Government's case for privatisation was based on

claims that private investors would be willing to pay a price for ETSA that exceeded its value in continued public ownership, and on arguments about the financial and other risks associated with participation in the National Electricity Market.

Quiggin and Spoehr in *Risky Business* (1998) criticised the government argument for failing to take account of retained earnings and other income derived from ETSA, and argued that a sale price of between $6 billion and $7 billion would be needed to offset the loss of income to the state associated with the sale or lease of electricity assets. Quiggin and Spoehr also criticised the government's claims regarding financial risks, and argued that the majority of electricity income was derived from the distribution and transmission sector, a low-risk natural monopoly. Projections of revenue, costs and profitability were presented. Chapter 3 evaluates many of these arguments in the light of experience since 1998.

The privatisation of the South Australian electricity industry has reduced the net worth of the public sector. South Australia is an electricity importer, so the bulk of the sale price (more than $4 billion out of a total of $5 billion) was realised through the sale of transmission and distribution assets. In the final year of public ownership, earnings before interest and tax were $368 million, of which the distribution and transmission assets contributed $300 million. In the absence of regulatory decisions that reduce the nominal return to these assets, the interest savings on the sale price will fall consistently short of the earnings foregone through privatisation. This is consistent with most Australian experience of privatisation.

Options for the future

The analysis presented above has identified substantial problems with the current structure of the electricity industry. On the other hand, a return to the old system of vertically integrated state-owned electricity supply industries does not seem feasible in the context of an emerging national grid.

In some respects, a return to policies that worked well in the past seems both feasible and appropriate. The natural monopoly components of the industry – transmission and distribution – should be restored to public ownership, with the individual states owning their own networks and the National Grid being jointly owned. The idea of competition between distribution networks should be abandoned. A single distribution network for each state would permit investment decisions to be guided by the needs of electricity users rather than by the strategic and regulatory considerations currently dominant.

Some reform of the pool system, which has been abandoned in most other jurisdictions, seems inevitable. In particular, it seems likely that long-term contracts will play a greater role in future. The challenge is to design contracts that provide adequate incentives for reserve capacity to enhance system reliability. The current system reflects an overreaction to the excess capacity of the late 1980s, and seems likely to produce repeated shortfalls in supply.

A judgement on the experiment with retail contestability is premature. However, consideration should be given to the problem of ensuring an adequate basic service for consumers who do not benefit from retail competition.

The final crucial requirement is the creation of explicit price incentives to reduce emissions of carbon dioxide and other greenhouse gases. This could take the form of a carbon tax as noted above, or the creation of tradeable emission permits. The latter approach would probably prove more palatable, since it is closer to the spirit of the current NEM.

Conclusion

The National Electricity Market is still developing. Some problems, however, are likely to become more rather than less acute. The Australian National Electricity Market commenced operation in a period of oversupply, so that problems of market power and excessive prices have not emerged until recently. It remains unclear whether an electricity auction market can produce adequate incentives for investment while generating appropriate prices for consumers. Similar problems are emerging in relation to the regulated monopoly component of the industry, the transmission and distribution sector. Regulators must set prices that do not reward inefficiency or allow monopoly profits, but nevertheless provide appropriate incentives for new investment. This is a delicate balance.

In the longer term, the problem of the environmental impact of an industry relying predominantly on carbon-based fuels remains to be addressed. A market solution would involve the creation of emissions credits which could be traded along with electricity in national markets. Although limited steps have been taken in this direction, much remains to be done.

References

Green, R J & Newbery, D M 1992, 'Competition in the British electricity spot market', *Journal of Political Economy*, vol. 100, no. 5, pp. 929–53.

Newbery, D M 1997, 'Pool reform and competition in electricity', paper presented to the IEA/LBS Lectures on Regulation Series VII, 11 November.

Quiggin, J 1995, 'Does privatisation pay?', *Australian Economic Review*, vol. 95, no. 2, pp. 23–42.

Quiggin, J & Spoehr, J 1998, 'ETSA', pp. 63–87 in J. Spoehr (ed.), *Risky Business: An independent assessment of the implications of the privatisation of public enterprise in South Australia*, Public Service Association of South Australia and the Centre for Labour Research, University of Adelaide, Adelaide.

Energy Issues and Challenges

CHAPTER 5

Understanding the National Electricity Market

ANDREW NANCE

Introduction

The internet stocks an extensive amount of information on the history and operation of the National Electricity Market (NEM). Taskforces have been convened, ministers have gained and lost related portfolios, the media constantly reports on and critiques this topic, and yet, to many, the NEM still remains somewhat of a mystery.

Since its inception in the mid- to late-1990s, the NEM has spawned a plethora of federal and state-based bodies with a range of responsibilities. The physical and institutional infrastructure that exists today is, to put it mildly, complicated. What follows is an attempt to demystify the NEM without dwelling on the complexities. For those who wish to investigate further, a list of some of the available internet resources has been provided.

With full retail contestability (FRC) due in South Australia in January 2003 and tariff increases of 25% announced, it is important to understand how we got to this point, why things changed, and what are some of the key issues. There is so much commentary and analysis surrounding the NEM that it is virtually impossible to take it all in. The language adopted here is deliberately conversational to facilitate an easy understanding of a complex issue.

To begin, we'll take a quick storybook look at electricity used around the home followed by an overview of the NEM. Next is a brief discussion of some of the economic theory underpinning the

NEM. By comparing the supply of electricity to something most people can grasp a little easier – the reticulation of water – the functioning of NEM will be explained. The chapter concludes with a look at how renewable energies like solar and wind fit into the market.

A short but eventful life

You've just got home from work, the air conditioner's on, you've just grabbed a drink for yourself and the kids from the fridge and some frozen left-overs from the freezer. You would have heard the fridge's compressor cut in if the kids hadn't already turned the TV on. Anyway, you pop the left-overs in the microwave and sit down to open the mail.

Electricity bill again? How much? Used how many units? When? What are they?

Well, the unit is a unit of energy and its real name is the kilowatt-hour.

A kilowatt-hour? How much is that?

Well, twenty minutes or so after walking in the door you just bought and used another one. Congratulations. It only cost you about 15 cents and they probably threw in a kilogram or so of greenhouse gases for free – not a bad deal.

Twenty minutes? That's not that long, there's a few of them in a day. No wonder it adds up.

And, of course, we all know they do.

The kilowatt-hour. They're great little things, you can buy them from your electricity retailer (probably AGL) and get them to do all sorts of stuff – cool your home, run your computer, keep your beer cold and your food fresh, give you light at night. Some people use them to get a hot shower, cook their food and heat water for the dishes.

If you are trying to understand the 'power crisis' and all the debate surrounding it, it may be useful for us to go on a journey with a kilowatt-hour. On this journey we will look at the life cycle of one kilowatt-hour. It was the one that lived that mere 20 minutes for us before. For the sake of this story we'll call that kilowatt-hour 'Killa'.

Killa's history can be traced back millions of years. Way back then Killa was probably a tree. Somehow Killa became buried, squashed and underwent the transformation into coal. This fossilised life was pretty uneventful until a series of explosions released him for a series of new adventures. Killa was in for more pain – being scooped up, beaten up, scrubbed, crushed and, finally, burnt. Reincarnated as a small amount of superheated steam, Killa was bashed against the blade of a turbine to help spin an electric generator. Two of Killa's friends were lost, wasted as heat, but for Killa, the lucky one in three who makes it, this led to the incarnation we knew so briefly – that neat, compact little packet of electrical energy produced by one of the generators at, in this case, Northern Power Station, near Port Augusta.

As soon as you turned on the air conditioner, the electricity began to flow – like water from a pipe. Meanwhile, the generator at the power station was busy pushing Killa and several other members of the 'watt' family into the other end of the pipe – just like a massive water pump. The generator charged about six cents at the market for Killa. That was the going rate at the National Electricity Market, the only market in town.

The only way Killa can get to your place is on the transmission and distribution network (the poles-and-wires bit). It's fast but a bit dangerous, like all roads. Some say one in ten go missing, lost, gone, never heard from again. Some disappear in the cables, some in the switchgear, some in the transformers. Killa's a bit nervous but quietly confident of making the journey successfully.

But you've got to pay to go on the network and there're plenty of meters along the way tracking Killa's every move. Retailer to the rescue – they'll make sure the toll is paid – you can fix them up later. The toll for Killa is about seven cents – one for the transmission business, ElectraNet, six for the distribution business, ETSA Utilities.

So, the journey has begun. Killa leaves the substation at Northern Power Station at high voltage – around 275,000 volts – necessary to squeeze all of Killa's mates in as well. This drops to around 66,000 volts as Killa gets closer to town and the 'watt' family begins to disperse. Then it's down to 11,000 volts as Killa reaches your neighborhood and down again to about 415 volts when Killa reaches your street. By the time Killa comes up your driveway, the familiar 240 volts applies.

The appropriately named kilowatt-hour meter in the meter box at your home flags his arrival – and advises AGL to add Killa to the list of kilowatt-hours you've bought this quarter and to add a final toll of about two cents. From here Killa is painlessly divided into the different circuits in your home. One bit is used to run the fridge, TV and microwave, another piece for lights and, maybe, another piece for the element in your hot water system or stove. Each of these devices uses their piece of Killa in a different way – heat, light, motion – whatever you want.

Fortunately, or unfortunately, depending on your point of view, the story of Killa and others members of the 'watt' family just plain happens – all you've got to do is pay.

However, imagine that Killa was a little round token, similar to a coin, and you had to keep filling your electricity meter with tokens as many of us have in past years for lights at a tennis or squash court or for a video or pinball game or a bumper-boat ride at Magic Mountain. Imagine further that someone explained to you that, with only a little effort, you could get nearly twice as much court time from each token, a free ball or a free game. Would you make the effort?

Well, the same applies to Killa but it's called 'energy efficiency' and it's something everyone should practise. For now though, we'll look a bit deeper into the NEM.

A brief history of the National Electricity Market

The National Electricity Market, or NEM, commenced trading on 13 December 1998 as a major part of the Australian power supply industry's deregulation process. A key objective of the NEM is the promotion of competition at each stage in the electricity generation-and-supply chain and this is consistent with the origins of its formation.

One of the earliest related events was Prime Minister Bob Hawke's 1991 'Building a Competitive Australia' statement in which a call was made for a 'national framework for competition policy and law'. This led to the report of the Independent Committee of Inquiry into National Competition Policy (the Hilmer Report) being presented to the Council of Australian Governments (COAG) in

1993 and eventually to the federal, state and territory governments agreeing to implement a National Competition Policy. This in turn led to the formation of the Australian Competition and Consumer Commission (ACCC) and the National Competition Council (NCC). These bodies have ongoing regulatory and oversight roles in the operation of the NEM. COAG has initiated a major review of energy markets in Australia which is due to report by early 2003.

Also in 1991, the Industry Commission released its report, *Energy Generation and Distribution* – leading to a National Grid Management Council investigation into the establishment of the National Grid and accompanying National Electricity Market. The identified potential for productivity and efficiency gains through restructuring the industry, particularly when incorporating principles of increased competition, assured the pursuit of the NEM.

It should be noted that none of the mandated reforms required privatisation of electricity assets. What was required however, was the disaggregation (or breaking-up) of the previously 'vertically inte-grated' electricity monopolies into separate functions (generation, transmission, distribution and retailing) and the 'corporatisation' (pursuit of 'corporate' management principles) within these elements. In SA this monopoly was ETSA. The transmission and distribution functions (the 'poles-and-wires' businesses) were and are considered 'natural monopoly' elements. This is simply recognition that there is no benefit to economic efficiency in having competing electricity grids – no one wanted to see two or more sets of poles and wires running down each street. Competition was however, mandated for the functions of generation and retailing and this is what we see today.

Through COAG, South Australia is party to a number of inter-governmental agreements which called for the restructure of the electricity supply industry and participation in the NEM. Significant funding from the Commonwealth to the states was conditional on effective implementation of the mandated reforms.

One of the first stages was the development of the 'market rules' – the National Electricity Code, referred to simply as 'the code'. Consequently, the National Electricity Code Administrator (NECA) was formed to monitor and enforce the code and the National Electricity Market Management Company (NEMMCO) to implement the code and 'operate' the system. (The five state governments are NEMMCO's shareholders and each government appoints a director to make up the NEMMCO board.) Any proposed code change requires ACCC authorisation under the *Trade Practices Act*. The ACCC looks at competition issues as well as at pricing and access to transmission networks (similar to another of its roles, that of monitoring interstate competition).

South Australia is one of four jurisdictions of the NEM and there are other regulatory responsibilities to be fulfilled at this level. Amongst other responsibilities, the Essential Services Commission (ESCOSA) (formerly the South Australian Independent Industry Regulator [SAIIR]) fulfils this regulatory role. The code also requires an annual planning review, including a 10-year forecast of supply, demand and system adequacy. This would have previously been an activity within (the integrated) ETSA, but following restructuring, the SA Electricity Supply Industry Planning Council (ESIPC) was formed to provide these forecasts. The Electricity Industry Ombudsman (EIO) scheme has also been established in SA to enhance consumer protection. The Office of the Technical Regulator (OTR) has also been formed (within Energy SA) to set and maintain technical and safety standards in the industry, a task, again, previously performed, to a large extent, by (the integrated) ETSA.

The businesses which operate the 'natural monopoly' elements (ElectraNet for high-voltage transmission and ETSA Utilities for the lower-voltage distribution) are heavily regulated in terms of prices charged and quality of service – by the ACCC for the transmission businesses and by ESCOSA for the distribution business.

To market, to market

At this stage it is important to emphasise that the physical side of electricity supply is pretty much the same as it always was. The market and the debate surrounding it relate to the way all the assets and functions are owned, managed, regulated and paid for. Before we look into the market's operation, we're going to look at some market theory and the model chosen for the NEM.

Most people are familiar with some form of market and have some concept of supply and demand. In basic form, markets are all about setting prices for a product or service. 'Free markets' are concerned with setting the 'right price'. The price for the product in the market place will be set by the balance of supply and demand. Ideally this price will equal what is known as the 'marginal cost' of production. The marginal cost of the product does not include any of the fixed costs associated with production, it just reflects the direct costs of producing it. Reaching marginal cost is regarded as an indication that the market is at its most efficient.

In order to reach the 'right price' in the market place, competition is required and the basic features of a competitive market are:

- many buyers and sellers, each with a small share of the trade
- transparent, complete and freely accessible information (to make the 'right decisions' about the 'right price')
- no restrictions on trading
- buyers and sellers able to vary their production or consumption in response to signals in the market.

So, how has this 'market theory' been applied to the buying and selling of electricity? The first step was to separate the buyers from the sellers: the generators were spun off into their own business, as the seller and the retail sales component became the buyer. Next step was to introduce some competition between the sellers – the generators. Several companies ended up with portfolios of power stations.

Next came competition between retailers, the buyers. Half a dozen different retailers are licensed and selling electricity to industrial and commercial customers and have been for a while. Full retail contestability represents the final group of customers able to choose which retailer buys electricity on their behalf.

One of the big decisions that had to be made early in the process was exactly how the transactions between buyers and sellers would occur. Australia chose to follow the UK model of the time, the wholesale pool, whereby all generators sell into the pool and receive the same 'spot' price, all retailers buy from the pool at the 'spot' price and then on-sell it. The 'spot' price is the going rate for electricity and reflects the willingness of the generators to sell their output. By only 'approving' the lowest bidders to generate electricity, the 'theory' of the market suggests a downward pressure on price all of the time.

As demand increases however, as on a hot summer's afternoon

when thousands of air conditioners are turned on, there are suffi-ciently few generators available to meet all of the demand. Thus they are able to command higher and higher prices. Nevertheless, some increase in price is legitimate under these circumstances and reflects increased costs of generation. Many of these generators are only called into operation for a few days each year, so their 'marginal cost' of production is higher than if they recovered their expenses over many more days as is the case with the 'baseload' plants.

So the wholesale pool has become the 'framework' for trading electricity. But in practice how well does it reflect the features of a competitive market described earlier? It could be argued that the present arrangements fail on all four features, one of the most fundamental being the extremely limited 'demand' response in the market. Referred to as 'inelasticity of demand', it means that we con-sumers 'buy' whatever electricity we want regardless of the price.

So the buyers display quite predictable behaviour and there is only limited competition between sellers (until the 'spot' price rises enough to get them interested). Such a context certainly makes for a seller's market. This is where 'regulation' fits in – to fill the gap between what really happens and what a 'free market' is supposed to deliver.

The wholesale pool model is certainly being questioned and, in the UK, has been relegated to dealing with only around 10% of the trade in electricity, the remainder being sold in separate contractual transactions between generators and retailers. There is a certain amount of contract-based trade in the NEM already and this is discussed briefly later in this chapter.

How does it work?
One of the key features of an electricity market that distinguishes it from other markets is the absence of storage – electricity is made when it is to be consumed. It is NEMMCO's responsibility to ensure the fine balance between supply and demand is maintained. If supply failed to meet demand, the voltage and frequency of the system would start to drop and household appliances and industry equipment would begin behaving erratically or even suffer perma-nent damage.

As stated, the model chosen for the NEM is that of a wholesale pool and the notion of a 'pool' of water provides a simple analogy for the NEM. Imagine that all of the water (electricity) is pumped into a bucket. Likewise, imagine that consumers draw all of their water from the same bucket. NEMMCO's responsibility is to ensure that the bucket never runs dry and never overflows, and to ensure that the cheapest generators get to sell the most.

Since there is no real storage in the realm of electricity grids (that is, the bucket doesn't hold much water compared to the amount flowing into or out of it), at five-minute intervals NEMMCO instructs (or 'despatches' in market terms) the generators to either start, stop or continue 'pumping'. Which generators get asked to 'pump' more water? The ones which have offered to deliver their water (electricity) at the lowest price. These may be interstate generators which pump their water (electricity) over a long pipeline – the interconnector. The NEM is itself identified as five regions (Qld, NSW, Snowy, Victoria and SA). Imagine then the NEM as five buckets all joined by these 'interconnector' pipelines that can move water from bucket to bucket.

As mentioned, the demand for electricity from the NEM is quite predictable and it is forecasted with reasonable accuracy (limited by the ability to predict the weather). Forecasting allows NEMMCO to plan for each day's requirements and for each generator to predict how much they can charge for their output and still get asked to supply – charge too much and you aren't asked to supply and you make no money, charge too little and you get asked to supply but know that you could have made more money.

Before we go any further one clear definition is required. This is the difference between a kilowatt and a kilowatt-hour (or megawatt and megawatt-hour). A kilowatt, expressed as kW, is a measure of power – the *rate* at which electricity is produced or consumed. A 1 kW array of solar panels (about five square metres) in full sun will *produce* electricity at a rate of 1000 watts (1 kW) in one hour. The typical household iron will *consume* electricity at about the same rate. If this production or consumption continues at the same rate for an hour, then the total *amount* of electric energy produced or consumed is one kilowatt-hour (expressed as kWh). Returning to the water analogy, it's the same difference as between flow *rate* (say, litres per minute) and *volume* (litres).

Generators bid daily into the NEM the amount of energy they are prepared to deliver at a given price. Again returning to the water analogy, a generator capable of delivering water to the bucket at up to 200 litres per minute would, for example, be prepared to deliver 100 litres per minute at a dollar a litre and a further 100 litres per minute at two dollars per litre. Initially, the bid of 100 litres per minute would be accepted and NEMMCO would 'dispatch' the generator to start pumping at that rate. At this point the going rate for water from the bucket is a dollar a litre. That's what the retailer pays and the generator gets paid.

As demand from the pool increases (people come home from work to water their lawns) and all of the 'dollar a litre' water is spoken for, a particular bid of another 100 may prove to be the next cheapest on offer. Thus NEMMCO would dispatch them again and they would increase supply but the going rate for water from the bucket now becomes this price; that is, the generator receives $2 for the entire amount of their water (now 200 litres per minute) as do all of the other generators pumping water to the bucket.

The interstate water being pumped over the pipeline is often relatively cheap but you can only squeeze so much water down the pipeline. Once this limit is reached (equivalent to a 'constrained' interconnector in the NEM), the price of water from the bucket can skyrocket. This is where 'peaking plant' are often called in. These can start pumping water very quickly but because they only get asked to do so a few days of the year they expect a greater price to cover their costs in doing so. Likewise, they have looked at the forecasts and notified NEMMCO that they are prepared to deliver, say, 50 litres per minute – the first 25 at $50 per litre, the second 25 at $100 – quite confident that there will be sufficient demand for their water, even at these prices, to be dispatched for long enough to cover their costs.

However, there is a cap on prices. This is referred to as the 'value of lost load' or VOLL (that is, what's the value to a consumer of their load being disconnected because there is insufficient electricity for everyone) and has been set at $10,000 per megawatt-hour (equal to $10 per kilowatt-hour, remembering household consumers pay around 15 cents for each kilowatt-hour). This is compared to recent average trading prices of around $20 to $40 (2–4 cents per kilowatt-hour). The increased return is necessary for the 'peaking plant' to generate sufficient return on their capital investment in the short time they have been delivering to the market but, interestingly, it is paid to all generators regardless of their cost to supply.

One of the more curious features of the market, and the one most often labelled as open to exploitation, is the practice of rebidding. The current market rules allow for generators to change their bids up to five minutes prior to despatch. The details of the rules are under review and change is imminent but, in short, the valid reasons for changing bids at short notice are quite broad and the potential exists for generators to withdraw capacity until demand meets available supply and the pool price rises, at which point they re-bid their capabilities at the higher price.

Another issue worth mentioning is the energy lost in the NEM's physical network of cables, transformers, switches and so. This is analogous to evaporation from the bucket and represents 5% to 10% of all of the generators' outputs. In short, consumers must buy up to 10% more electricity from generators than they end up being able to use and this is accommodated by the NEM's settlement process.

Someone has to own, operate and maintain the pipelines to and from the bucket and, in the NEM, these businesses are referred to as the network service providers or NSPs. To continue with the water theme, imagine the high-pressure pipelines between the generators and the bucket as the NEM's transmission network (operated by transmission NSPs such as SA's ElectraNet) and the low-pressure pipelines leaving the bucket and carrying water to the consumers as the NEM's distribution network (operated by distribution NSPs such as SA's ETSA Utilities). The NSPs of course need to be paid and this payment comprises the majority of a consumer's bill and reflects the capital- and maintenance-intensive nature of these businesses.

There are two ways to stop the bucket running dry – pump more water into it or draw less from it. The latter is what's broadly referred to as demand-side-management (DSM). It should be apparent by now that everyone pays the same price for their water from the bucket, so there can be overall cost benefits if one of the large consumers offers to draw less water, for a payment of, say, 50 cents a litre, to prevent an otherwise inevitable price rise of, say, a dollar a litre as we saw before. When this is done in the market, it is referred to as demand-side-participation or DSP. It is, however, rare.

All dollars, no cents?

Although we're all physically connected all the way back to the generators, we don't all trade. Small users like the average household or small business get a retailer to trade for them. At present, the price charged by the retailer is determined under the electricity pricing order (EPO) and has been reviewed annually by the industry regulator in consultation with others. From January 2003, the EPO will no longer be applied to retailers and customers must negotiate a price with the retailer. These prices will have to be justified to the satisfaction of the Essential Services Commission.

As we have seen, the retailer is exposed to the wholesale pool and its volatile prices. The retailer endeavours to insulate customers from these price variations but has a number of (mainly financial) instruments at hand to minimise the risk of paying more for power than they have agreed with their customers to sell it. This is one reason why tariffs are expected to rise after January 2003.

The popular method available to retailers at present for managing risk is the 'hedge contract'. Typically this is a two-way agreement between retailers and generators in which a price is agreed for a certain amount of electricity. This is known as the 'strike' price. The electricity is traded in the wholesale pool as normal, but the generator and retailer compensate each other when the spot price differs from the strike price. If the retailer had to pay more than the strike price, the generator 'refunds' the difference. Alternatively, if the retailer is able to buy at a spot price below the strike price, the generator is refunded the difference. These 'refunds' occur outside the NEM and as a result, limited details exist of the amount of electricity covered by such contracts, but this is certainly a sanctioned – in fact an encouraged – activity. The actual price paid for electricity is therefore the net balance of the strike price for the quantity under contract and the spot price paid for electricity outside contract coverage.

The market rules also allow for similar arrangements between the generators and other end-use customers and some commentators advocate this as a preferred model for the entire market – avoiding the 'pool' altogether. The UK's New Electricity Trading Arrangements (NETA) follow this philosophy: around 90% of wholesale electricity is traded 'under contract' with the balance purchased in the power exchanges.

So, how does settlement occur in the NEM? Each day consists of 48 trading blocks of a half-hour each. Each of these half-hours contains six dispatch intervals of five minutes each. The price for each dispatch interval is that of the highest bid that was dispatched (or, to put it another way, the cheapest combination of generator bids that, when combined, met the demand for electricity). The 'spot' or 'clearing' price for a given half-hour interval is determined as the average of the prices set during these six five-minute dispatch intervals. It is worth noting that different prices are set for each of the NEM regions although they are normally quite similar. Price differences between regions make it worthwhile to transfer power across an interconnector but, as described earlier, when no more transfer can occur, local generators will set (and benefit from) the trading price.

So where does all the money go? Well, in rough terms, NEMMCO states that, of the final price paid by end-use consumers, about 35% goes to the generators, 60% to the NSPs (12% for transmission and 48% for distribution) and about 5% goes to the retailer. Out of this money various other parties are paid for a myriad of services necessary for the operation of the system, some relating to technical aspects, others to administrative.

The trading prices are available, in real time, over the internet at NEMMCO's website – www.nemmco.com.au and may make for fascinating entertainment from the comfort of your air-conditioned home or office on day four of a heat wave! This site also contains an enormous amount of other information on the operation of the NEM.

Who used what? When?

The previous discussion has made it clear that the price of electricity varies during a day, and from one day to the next and certainly from season to season. So an electricity retailer's cost incurred buying the electricity which is on-sold to your household or business is quite variable. However, the selling price to you is a fixed rate by volume sold, regardless of when the retailer bought the electricity you used. The familiar example used to illustrate this is the reverse-cycle air conditioner. On a hot afternoon, thousands of these units start up and add to the thousands still operating in offices and industry. The resultant demand for electricity can be almost double that of other times. Your retailer will be paying much more for your electricity than is able to sell it to you.

Due to the very simple metering system installed in homes and small businesses, it is not known exactly who is using how much when – only how much has been used since the last time the meter was read. The only option for retailers under these circumstances is to add up all of these times when they are paying more than they sell for and spread the costs across all customers. Put simply, everyone's electricity costs more because of the large number of refrigerant air conditioners in this state, a rather tragic situation for many low-income households.

However, larger customers have more intelligent metering systems installed which record what they use and when. The less 'peaky' their daily load profile is, the better chance they have of securing a good price in their electricity contract. They can also reduce the amount they pay in network charges if they can avoid heavy consumption during these summer peak periods.

The equivalent metering for households is seen by many commentators as essential for the entire 'market' to operate like a 'real market', one characterised by both supply *and* demand. More sophisticated and sensitive metering can allow tariffs to send a clear signal to people that they can pay less for their energy if they manage their demand for it.

There has been much debate over the merits of this 'time-of-use' metering for residential customers. The balance of opinion from retailers, regulators, environmentalists and consumer advocates seems to be that 'smart meters' for all would send the right signals for energy efficiency and improve the transparency of the market. But, attracting long-term investment from the private sector seems unlikely since no one in South Australia wants to take responsibility for the provision of 700,000 meters. Widespread roll-out of smart meters has occurred in Italy, parts of the US and elsewhere. Their increased utilisation will eventually reduce their cost even further.

Where does renewable energy fit in?

Renewable energy (such as that derived from solar, wind, hydro-electric and biomass generators) is 'traded' in two distinct ways. First, there's the 'GreenPower' schemes offered by electricity retailers such as AGL in SA. Customers pay a premium tariff to be assured that AGL has sourced the equivalent of their electricity consumption from an accredited renewable energy source. Second, there's the electricity that must be sourced to comply with the federal government's mandatory renewable energy target (MRET or '2%' legislation).

The MRET and 'GreenPower' programs both aim to reduce greenhouse gas emissions from electricity generation and drive investment in renewable energy projects. However, MRET is a federal mandatory requirement and retailers are fined if they do not reach their targets. GreenPower on the other hand, relies on voluntary participation by consumers and aims to ensure the viability of renewable energy projects over and above what is required to satisfy the MRET obligations.

There are differences in eligibility requirements also, and, in general terms, 'GreenPower' is slightly 'greener' than necessary to satisfy MRET requirements. These differences are mainly in the details of including various biomass-fuelled (plant-based material used in either a solid, liquid or gaseous form) generators. Many environmental groups have criticised the MRET legislation for its inclusion of large-scale hydroelectric projects and 'waste' from 'managed' native forest activities, both of which 'GreenPower' excludes.

Before we go a little deeper into each program, just how much power are we talking about? The national MRET target for 2002 is

1100 GWh (that's gigawatt-hours, each of which is equal to one million kilowatt-hours) while the nation's 60,000 'GreenPower' customers are expected to consume somewhere around 500 GWh in 2002. To put this in perspective, South Australia's households, businesses and government operations will use somewhere around 11,000 GWh in 2002 out of the combined NEM states which will consume in the order of 150,000 GWh. So, the combined renewable energy under these two schemes represents an equivalent of about 1% of the electricity traded in the NEM. Although the schemes are driving reasonable levels of investment in renewable projects, many environmental, industry and political groups are calling for much larger targets to be set.

GreenPower

GreenPower is an accreditation program that sets quite strict environmental standards for renewable energy products offered by electricity retailers to households and businesses across Australia. The NSW Government's Sustainable Development Authority (SEDA) launched the program in 1997 as part of its mandate to drive investment in renewable energy by increasing consumer confidence in, and demand for, 'green' electricity.

The popularity and success of the program has seen it expand to become a national initiative 'steered' by the energy agencies of the NEM governments. In SA this is Energy SA which is also responsible for 'accrediting' local products.

AGL offers an accredited product to its South Australian customers but, unfortunately, participation to date in SA has been low with only around 300 customers reported in 2001 out of the national total of around 60,000. AGL sources the energy from a landfill site and some smaller biomass generators. With sufficient demand it is hoped that some of the proposed wind power projects in South Australia may also be engaged in the scheme.

The GreenPower products are flexible, with customers generally able to choose to purchase all or a proportion of their electricity as renewable electricity. In SA the premium is around 4c per kWh (plus GST of course) or 25% more than 'standard' or 'fossil' electricity.

Overall, GreenPower electricity is sourced from solar and wind projects (about 10%), biomass (about 45%) and hydroelectric projects (about 45%). Further information can be obtained from www.greenpower.com.au and AGL's website at www.agl.com.au.

Mandatory Renewable Energy Target (MRET)

The *Renewable Energy (Electricity) Act 2000* introduced the MRET on 1 April 2001, requiring electricity retailers (such as AGL) and other wholesale buyers to purchase an additional 9500 GWh of renewable energy nationwide by 2010. Again, to put this in perspective, this is equivalent to about two-thirds of the projected electricity demand in SA for 2010, which is a significant amount of electricity, but remember, SA consumes less than 8% of the nation's electricity!

It is also worth noting that, if growth in overall energy consumption to 2010 reaches recent forecasts, simply meeting the target quantity may mean an overall reduction in the proportion of energy derived from renewable sources in Australia! Such growth rates would however, only result from failing to implement many of the cost-effective energy-efficiency opportunities available to consumers.

In order to verify compliance with the legislation, another government agency has been established – the Office of the Renewable Energy Regulator (ORER). This body manages a reasonably innovative scheme that requires each retailer (on behalf of their large customers) to surrender a certain number of 'renewable energy certificates' or RECs to the ORER on Valentine's Day each year as proof they have met the interim targets set for them based on the volume of electricity they purchase.

Each REC represents one megawatt-hour of electricity (equal to 1000 kilowatt-hours) which is also the trading unit of the NEM wholesale pool. The cost of not surrendering the required amount of RECs is $40 each – roughly the average price of electricity traded in the NEM. RECs are created, registered and traded on the internet and are not just the domain of these large retailers. Install a solar hot-water system or some photovoltaic (solar-electric) panels at your home and you are also eligible to a specific number of RECs that, typically, a retailer will buy from you for around $25 each. The principle behind this scheme is that, by making use of the sun at your home, you 'displace' the use of 'fossil-fuel'-based electricity that would have otherwise been required from the grid. In the case of solar water heaters for example, the amount of electricity *not* used over the life of the heater (about 10 years) is estimated and you are entitled to the equivalent RECs upfront at the time of installation. This can be worth in the order of $700 for 'family-size' domestic systems, which, it is hoped, will encourage the uptake of these technologies.

The ORER's website contains a large amount of additional information and can be accessed at www.orer.gov.au.

Useful internet sites
Government

CoAG (Council of Australian Governments) – energy market review, available at www.energymarketreview.org

Federal Department of Industry, Tourism and Resources, available at www.industry.gov.au

AGO (Australian Greenhouse Office), available at www.greenhouse.gov.au

Energy SA, available at www.energy.sa.gov.au

SEDA (NSW Sustainable Energy Development Authority), available at www.seda.nsw.gov.au

Regulation

ACCC, Australian Competition and Consumer Commission available at www.accc.gov.au

ESCOSA, Essential Services Commission of South Australia available at www.escosa.sa.gov.au

NECA, National Electricity Code Administrator available at www.neca.com.au

OTR, Office of the Technical Regulator available at www.energysafety.sa.gov.au

ORER, Office of the Renewable Energy Regulator available at www.orer.gov.au

Operation/planning

NEMMCO, National Electricity Market Management Company
available at www.nemmco.com.au

ESIPC, Electricity Supply Industry Planning Council available at
www.esipc.sa.gov.au

Ombudsman

EIO, Electricity Industry Ombudsman available at www.eiosa.com.au

CHAPTER 6

Electricity Markets, Competition and Prices

Myths and realities

CHRIS FINN

Introduction: The NEM vision

The competitive restructuring of the National Electricity Market (NEM) was premised upon two fundamental beliefs: first, it was assumed that competitive pressures in the generation sector and, to a lesser extent, in the retail sector of the electricity supply industry would exert sufficient downward pressure on prices to keep them at economically efficient levels. Second, it was believed that pressure from remote generators located interstate and the supply of power via the National Grid would act to smooth out price imbalances between the various NEM jurisdictions, thus creating a truly 'national' market providing 'cheap' electricity for both industrial and domestic consumers.

South Australia in particular, has not conformed to these high expectations. First of all, the relatively small size of the South Australian market has meant that competition between generators, muted at best throughout the NEM, has been particularly weak in South Australia. The weakness has been exacerbated by the ability and willingness of generators, both in SA and other NEM regions, to use their undoubted market power to 'game' the market and set pool prices well above competitive levels. Second, difficulties in securing adequate interconnection capacity between SA and the rest of the NEM has meant that, at the times of greatest need, and with little reserve generation capacity, the state finds itself virtually isolated and unable to benefit fully from cheaper interstate generation capacity. The result, with full retail competition looming in 2003, is that South Australian consumers are particularly exposed to the likelihood of significant price rises.

Critics of NEM reforms are often accused of ignoring the long-term ability of a market to correct itself. Thus, it is argued, market manipulations by generators are correctly seen simply as price signals indicating a market opportunity for investment in new generation capacity. This new generation capacity, it is suggested, will allay the potential for market abuse and bring prices back to more competitive levels. In short, the market will sort itself out and any form of regulatory intervention is only likely to delay that process occurring.

Sadly, this argument has serious defects. Crucially, it takes price rises as the 'natural' effects of supply-and-demand imbalances. However, they are nothing of the sort. Rather, supply-and-demand balances in the NEM regions can be, and are, manipulated at will by generators withdrawing capacity or pricing it at artificially high levels which bear no relationship at all to the costs of production. At the same time, generators are entirely capable of lowering costs in the short term in order to deter new investment which threatens their position. Thus, even high spot prices in the compulsory pool, due to their instability, are less than reliable price signals for potential new investors.

It might also be observed that even where new entry does occur, market forces are still insufficient to force competitive behaviour. On the contrary, new entrants may simply choose to mimic the market manipulations of their purported 'competitors'. There is already evidence of quasi-collusive bidding practices in the NEM.

Finally, it is reasonable to ask just how much in the way of higher prices consumers ought to be asked to bear in order to send 'price signals' to the 'market'. The NEM design hoped to use the spot market both as a method of achieving allocative efficiency in the production and pricing of electricity, and as a way of signalling the need for new investment. It is becoming clear that these goals are in conflict. At best, the market might be expected to follow a 'boom and bust' cycle in investment with periods of oversupply and lower prices leading to a drying-up of investment. As demand grew, this would in turn result in supply shortfalls and consequent leaps in prices. Only then might 'the market' respond with significant investment in new generation capacity. In order to avoid the disruptions inherent in such a cycle it may be necessary to return to a measure of coordination and planning in the development of both new generation and new transmission capacity. A further difficulty is that the majority of new investment which has appeared in the NEM has been in gas-fired 'peaking' plant. Additional cheaper 'baseload' capacity, which would tend to exert downward pressure on pool prices, has been slow to emerge.

South Australia and the National Electricity Market

South Australia finds itself in a particularly invidious position in the NEM. Being a small market, there is only very limited competition between generators located within the state. South Australia has quite limited numbers of generators, particularly of directly comparable technical characteristics. Generators of quite different technical characteristics can only compete to a very limited extent. In addition, there is only limited competition available from remote generation in other states as interconnection capacity is limited. Transmission losses also add to the cost of imported power, limiting its ability to undercut locally sourced generation. Finally, it should be noted that manipulation of pool prices in other NEM regions means that they cannot necessarily be relied upon as a moderately cheap alternative source of electricity, particularly at periods of peak demand.

To expand on these issues let us look closely at the existing generation capacity in the state. South Australia has only two true baseload generators, with a combined capacity of about 660 MW. Given that baseload plants have the lowest operating costs, but are slow to start up and stand down, these two plants operate at all times and bid low into the market in order to be assured of being scheduled by National Electricity Market Management Company (NEMMCO), the market manager. They are thus scheduled first. The two baseload plants are not significantly constrained by one another as demand within the state will always exceed their combined capacity. In practice, they can always bid up to the marginal price of the next available unit of capacity without losing sales as a consequence.

The baseload plants would usually be followed by electricity supplied over the existing Heywood interconnector located in the south-east of the state. This combination would give a total capacity of 1160 MW. In practice, however, this will not always occur, as higher pool prices in Victoria may mean that additional generation capacity within South Australia is cheaper and will be scheduled first.

The recently commissioned Pelican Point cogeneration plant supplies a further 450 MW of power, giving a total capacity of 1610 MW. However, the next 1280 MW of capacity is supplied by the Torrens Island Power Station. As summer demand ranges from around 1200 MW to 2000 MW with peaks of 2500 MW or higher, this means that Torrens Island will be the marginal generator throughout that range. It can set the price, anywhere between about $30/MWh and $150/MWh, without encountering price competition from peaking plant. In short, it has market power through a significant demand range. It is not significantly constrained by competing generators and has a great deal of freedom in the manner in which it chooses to bid its electricity into the pool. If peaking plant is required, usually due to outages, then the pool price can spike into the $4000–$5000 range. When this happens, however, it is not always due simply to very high demand. On the contrary, major generators are free under the NEM rules to withdraw significant amounts of otherwise available capacity from the market, thus forcing NEMMCO to call upon much higher priced capacity. Given the marginal pricing mechanism which applies to the pool (all generators receive the 'spot' price; that is, the price of the highest priced bid called upon), generators can actually make much larger profits by offering reduced quantities of electricity for sale.

Thus, even if generators had every intention of acting as competitively as possible in South Australia, there is simply very little competitive pressure upon them. Each performs within the range of its own technical characteristics. Within that range there is a lack of the competitive pressure which might force generators to bid at their marginal cost in order to be scheduled. Rather, the lack of direct competition allows a generator to engage in 'Bertrand' bidding; that is, bidding its capacity at a price just below the marginal price of the next class of generator in the merit order. This is hardly the result contemplated in the original conception of the NEM. In fact, however, bidding practices may be even less restrained than this, as there is little pressure forcing the 'next' generator to itself bid at its own marginal cost.

After a relatively mild summer in 2001–02 a disturbing trend began to emerge in the bids offered into the NEM pool in May and June 2002. After the VOLL (volume of lost load – see explanation of term in previous chapter) price (the maximum price for bids) was raised from $5000/MWh to $10,000 in April 2002, pool prices rose dramatically. The new maximum of $10,000/MWh was reached for the first time in July 2002. Significantly, these pool price rises were not a result of peak demands for electricity in winter-peaking regions such as New South Wales. Reserve capacity margins were adequate throughout this period. In fact, the high pool prices were entirely attributable to the bidding behaviour of a number of large generators. These generators simply bid large quantities of their available capacity into the market at very high prices of $4000/MWh or higher. When that capacity was called upon by NEMMCO to meet demand, the pool price inevitably spiked to those very high levels. There would seem to be no real economic justification for such high-priced bids of baseload and intermediate generation capacity. On the contrary, such bids simply reflect the existence and use of generator market power. They seem a far cry from the National Competition Policy vision of a strongly competitive National Electricity Market. South Australia, as already seen in the summer of 2000–01 is equally vulnerable to this form of market manipulation, which makes a mockery of attempts to project the adequacy of supplies in meeting demand.

Legal and regulatory constraints: The pool rules

It is useful to consider briefly what legal and regulatory constraints exist in the NEM, in particular, is there anything in the regulatory regime which might act as a surrogate for competitive forces and therefore constrain bidding behaviour? The short answer is no. The market rules are contained in the voluminous National Electricity Code. As part of the implementation process for the NEM, this code was 'authorised' by the ACCC under part VII of the

Commonwealth Trade Practices Act 1974. The effect of this authorisation is that anticompetitive conduct, other than misuse of market power, which might otherwise be seen as a breach of that act is provided with legal immunity. In a nutshell, the extraordinary result is that, despite the significance of the NEM to Australian domestic and industrial consumers, most anticompetitive conduct within that industry will not amount to a breach of the act. Nor does the exclusion of 'misuse of market power' from the authorisation process mean that generator-bidding practices may be challenged on this basis. As it happens, the definition of such misuse in the act is such that generator-bidding behaviour, although clearly anticompetitive, is very unlikely to fall within the prohibition. Most of the bidding behaviour of generators, including withdrawing capacity simply to manipulate the pool price, engaging in economic withholding through pricing capacity at extremely high levels, or rebidding available capacity between various price bands at the last possible moment prior to despatch, is simply not prohibited.

The national code, of course, provides its own rules governing the behaviour of market participants, including generators. These are the 'market rules' which govern the behaviour of all market participants including generators. However, the code is itself almost entirely devoid of provisions which deal with abuse of market power by generators, particularly via their rebidding practices. The key regulator, the National Electricity Code Administrator has only once taken action for a breach of the bidding rules, resulting in a civil penalty of a paltry $10,000 being paid by the infringing generator. In general, neither the code nor the *Trade Practices Act* even purports to constrain the undoubted market power of generators. It is left to 'market forces' to generate competitive efficiencies. But these are muted at best, and nowhere more so than in South Australia.

More competition within South Australia and the NEM?

This chapter suggests that the heart of the problem in South Australia, and indeed in the NEM as a whole, lies in the small size of the generation market, and the relatively large proportion of each segment of that market controlled by individual generators. As we have seen, this means that there is very little competition, except perhaps between peaking plant. Baseload and intermediate plant are largely unconstrained. Overseas experience suggests that, given the unusual nature of electricity as a product which cannot be stored and which requires the instantaneous fine balancing of supply and demand, even 20 or 30 directly competing generation units are insufficient. The United Kingdom was unable to achieve competitive outcomes with nearly 40 generators supplying into a pool, and ultimately abandoned the pool model for pricing electricity. Scandinavian experience suggests that a pool may be a viable option, with approximately 200 generators exerting competitive pressure upon one another. Clearly, this is not a viable option within South Australia in the foreseeable future, or indeed within the NEM as a whole.

The possibilities of competition are further reduced when we consider the limited reserve margins existing in South Australia. Of all the NEM regions, South Australia has probably the lowest reserve margins. This means that, in times of peak demand, virtually all available capacity must be scheduled to meet that demand. Thus, the possibility of unreasonably high bid prices being undercut by the offers of another local generator are remote. There is simply not sufficient reserve capacity within the state to allow this possibility. High bids therefore can go virtually unconstrained by supply-side competition. The situation is only exacerbated when generators manipulate the supply-and-demand balance by unilaterally with-drawing capacity from the market or simply bidding that capacity at very high price levels. In such circumstances, NEMMCO will have no alternative, under the present market rules, but to schedule those very high-priced bids. Given the marginal pricing mechanism within the pool, all generators will then make substantial windfall profits which have nothing to do with rewards for effective competition. Overseas experience, for example in California, suggests that reserve margins of at least 20% are required in order to exert significant competitive pressure on generators and to restrain their bids at or around marginal levels. Reserve margins in the NEM, and South Australia in particular, are set at much lower levels than this, at around 5–6%. These are set at a level designed to preserve system security, rather than to provide for competitive pressure.

One approach might have been, at the time of privatisation, to break generators into much smaller units. Although breaking each power station down into individual turbines, each offering their product to the pool separately, seems a very complex solution to the problem, it would at least greatly increase the degree of competition at the baseload and intermediate levels. However, at the time of privatisation, the South Australian Government's priority was clearly to maximise sale prices, and the prospect of enhanced profitability for the purchasers of generation assets was the key to this. Here, the short-term political imperatives of the budget bottom line clearly triumphed over a more sober assessment of the long-term interests of South Australian electricity consumers. Cash in the coffers was seen as more important than vigorous and effective competition.

The alternative to competition between generators within South Australia is competition from outside the state. The 'vision' of the National Electricity Market was underpinned by the concept of a truly national grid. With this grid in place, electricity could be sourced from anywhere in the NEM. Thus, higher-priced South Australian generation capacity would face strong competition from remote generators located in Victoria, New South Wales and even Queensland. Although such remote generation would suffer the cost disadvantage of transmission losses, this was potentially out-weighed by the much cheaper fuel sources available to some of these generators. Thus, under the NEM vision, generators throughout the NEM regions would find themselves much smaller players in a much bigger market and experience strong competitive pressure from each other, forcing prices bid into the spot market to remain at the lowest viable levels, throughout the country.

Sadly, this national grid simply does not exist. It has not been built. The Australian electricity market remains a prisoner of its history and, to some extent, of the division of powers within the Australian Constitution. Historically, each of the Australian states developed its own electricity system, with only limited interconnection between them. Often, in a manner analogous to difficulties with railway gauges, they adopted different transmission voltages, a fact which increases the difficulties and energy losses associated with linking the separate state systems. This was the system inherited by the NEM.

Subsequent progress towards the physical creation of a truly national market has been slow. South Australia still has only limited interconnection with the rest of the NEM. The Heywood interconnector supplies up to 500 MW of power from Victoria. At times of peak demand, however, where the pool price spikes dramatically upwards, it may be constrained and reach the limit of its capacity. Once this happens, South Australia is effectively separated from the rest of the NEM. A new unregulated interconnector, Murraylink, comes into operation in 2002. However, the development of the 'Riverlink' line from New South Wales to South Australia has been a saga illustrative of much that is unsatisfactory with the NEM.

In order to proceed as a regulated transmission line, thereby receiving a regulated rate of return, an interconnector project must undertake a regulatory approval process and pass a 'regulatory test' approved by the ACCC. The exact nature of this test has been an ongoing bone of contention. The test has been altered once, and was now the subject of further review by the ACCC in 2002. Rather astonishingly, the current formulation of the test does not directly address the issue of whether increased interconnection capacity would result in stronger competitive forces operating in the downstream market, for example, in South Australia. Given that the role of remote generation in ramping up competitive pressures was pivotal to the NEM vision, this is an astounding omission.

When the Riverlink project was first put forward for regulatory approval in 1998, the proposal did not pass the regulatory test as it was then formulated. This was one of the catalysts for the subsequent modification of that test in 1999. The project was finally approved in 2001, but is not expected to come into operation until 2005.

Riverlink was also the victim of a lack of support from the state government. Again, the desire to maximise the financial return from the privatisation process was the key here. South Australian generation assets were simply worth more to private investors if their pricing outcomes were not threatened by interstate competition. The budgetary considerations underpinning the sale process were again directly at odds with the policy goals of a competitive National Electricity Market. South Australian consumers may have had a short-term gain on the state government balance sheet, but they are likely to be paying the long-term cost in increased electricity prices for the foreseeable future. Indeed, the need for the new owners of generation plant, both in South Australia and in Victoria, to service their debt is one of the forces driving their bidding strategies in the NEM.

What has happened to prices in the NEM?

There is a multitude of conflicting claims relating to the effects of competitive restructuring upon electricity prices. The NEM, it seems, has been everything from an outstanding success to an abject failure. There are at least three reasons for these confusions. First, the timeframe is significant. Electricity prices, like the stock market, have both risen and fallen over time, which means that start and end dates for measurement become highly significant. Second, it is important to distinguish between wholesale 'pool' prices – the prices fixed initially by 'vesting' and more recently by 'hedging' contracts – and the retail prices paid by different classes of consumers. Third, once price variations have been identified it is important to pick out their causes.

An Australian Bureau of Agricultural Research (ABARE) study released in 2001 concluded that significant increases in productivity in the generation sector in particular had occurred from 1991 to 1999. Increases in labour productivity, directly attributable to 'down-sizing' were a major contributor here. The fact that the study calculated gains from 1991 indicates that it included improvements which occurred prior to, although perhaps in anticipation of, the beginning of the NEM at the end of 1998. The study commented that, as a result of both these productivity gains, and due to the existence of excess generation capacity, the wholesale price of electricity had declined significantly when compared with previous arrangements. It is notable, however, that the ABARE study did not draw directly on pool price data in order to reach its conclusions. Rather, it focussed on increased rates of labour and capital productivity without assuming that those increases were necessarily passed on as reduced wholesale pool prices and ultimately as reduced retail prices for end consumers. In fact, the study went on to note that the market power of generators was contributing to pool prices being set at levels consistently higher than those that might be expected under more competitive conditions.

So what has happened to wholesale pool prices in the NEM? There is little doubt that these did decline in the early days of the NEM, due to the degree of excess capacity that existed at that time, particularly in New South Wales and Queensland. However, the position is complex. The greatest declines occurred in Queensland in early 1999, immediately upon the commencement of the spot market. Prices then doubled over the following summer period before falling again in the second quarter of 2000. A further decline occurred in the second quarter of 2001, until a sudden jump in May and June of 2002. In New South Wales, prices were initially much lower than those in Queensland. They rose steadily until late in 2000, then underwent a series of fluctuations, falling to their lowest levels since market commencement. However, since May 2002 they have doubled from their previous levels. The trend in Victoria has been very similar to that in NSW, perhaps reflecting the significant level of interconnection between the two, which allows equalisation of pool prices.

South Australian pool prices have followed a somewhat different path. These were initially lower than prices in Queensland but rose within a few months of market start, while those in Queensland fell dramatically. Prices in South Australia remained substantially higher than those in other NEM regions throughout the first year of the NEM but approached overall NEM levels in mid-2000 before rising much more steeply than others over the 2000–01 summer. They again equalised in mid-2001 and stayed comparable to other regions through the mild summer of 2001–02. Along with the other NEM regions, pool prices in South Australia rose sharply in May and June 2002 to about twice their level of only three months previously.

It is apparent that claims about the overall trend in wholesale prices are highly dependent upon the timeframe chosen. Pool prices fell initially in all regions except in South Australia, where they rose sharply. By the end of December 2001 it was possible to say that they had fallen in all regions, including South Australia, and the mild summer that followed meant that both demand and pool prices stayed unexpectedly low. However, sharp rises in May and June

2002 meant that, by 30 June 2002, prices in NSW and Victoria were at about twice the levels which applied at NEM start-up and those in South Australia and Queensland were also moving sharply upwards. It was perhaps ominous that the highest spot price ever recorded in the NEM up to the 30 June 2002, a peak of $8049/MWh, occurred in New South Wales on that date. The National Electricity Code Administrator's (NECA) statistical summary of the April-to-June quarter noted that bidding activity seen in NSW and Queensland through May and June added almost a third to the overall average prices for 2001–02 for those regions.

The final point to be made about wholesale prices is that they are not just dependent upon the productive efficiency of labour and capital but also on input fuel costs. Cheaper coal and gas prices will potentially lower wholesale electricity prices, regardless of the competitive restructuring that has occurred in the NEM. Higher input prices will of course have the opposite effect. One of the difficulties with NEM design is ensuring that there are sufficient competitive pressures at work on generators that any gains they may make from lower fuel input costs are passed on via lower pool prices and not simply captured as windfalls.

It has been argued above that pool prices may not necessarily reflect the underlying cost structures of generators, as they are insufficiently exposed to competitive pressures. It is also true that retail prices are not simply a reflection of those attained in the pool. This is due to the ability of retailers to cushion, at least to some extent, the impact of pool price rises via hedging contracts between themselves and generators. To the extent that market players are hedged, a generator derives no financial benefit from high pool prices and a retailer pays no more. The difficulty for a retailer lies in actually securing an adequate level of hedge cover. Anecdotal evidence suggests that this is becoming increasingly difficult as generators seek to profit from their ability to manipulate pool prices upwards beyond competitive levels. Given this ability, it is in the interests of generators to limit the amount of capacity they are willing to offer as hedges to retailers. Higher returns can be obtained by selling directly via the pool. Where generators are willing to make capacity available for hedging purposes it is reasonable to assume that a premium will apply to the contract price. This is the premium paid by the retailer, and eventually passed on to the consumer, for the smoothing of risk that the hedge contract provides. In short, the risk generated by the market behaviour of generators can be alleviated by hedging, but only at a price. Inevitably, hedging contracts are negotiated in the shadow of the ability of generators to manipulate pool prices upwards. It is a negotiation in which the retailers find themselves in much the weaker bargaining position.

What then have been the trends in retail prices? A Productivity Commission study of infrastructure price trends, based on Australian Bureau of Statistics figures and released in 2002 concluded that retail metropolitan household electricity prices were lower in 2000–01 than they were in 1990–2001, with the exceptions of Adelaide, Hobart and Canberra. In Adelaide, these prices were 9% higher. The study suggested that rebalancing of tariff structures between access and usage, in line with 'user pays' approaches was a key reason for the rise in Adelaide. However, there was little detailed examination of the basis for the result.

A number of comments can be made. First, as with the ABARE study, the time base chosen long predates the existence of the NEM. Thus, it is far from apparent that trends upwards in South Australia, or trends downwards interstate, can be attributed simply or directly to the influence of the national market. In South Australia, it appears that prices fell from 1990 till about 1996 when the 'rebalancing' of tariff structures occurred. Since then, they have moved upwards. Prices in all capitals increased in the last year of the study, due to the effect of the GST. Second, this study does not take into account the potential longer-term effects on retail prices of the sudden and sharp rise in pool prices observed in May and June 2002. Should this trend be maintained, the impact will be felt not simply via the pool price but also in the prices for new hedging agreements between generators and retailers. Finally, it should be noted that full retail competition commenced only in January 2002 in Victoria and New South Wales (at a time of comparatively low pool prices) and commences in South Australia only in January 2003. Until those dates, the majority of consumers, particularly domestic consumers, benefitted from the combination of vesting contracts and regulated retail prices. Once full retail competition is implemented, all consumers are exposed, albeit indirectly, to the unknowns of the pool price and its fluctuations. At the very least, this is likely to result in risk premiums being built into hedge contract prices and then passed on to consumers. Where hedging is not available, or only available in limited quantities, retailers will have little alternative but to build risk premiums into their own margins.

The effects of retail contestability have varied considerably over time, between classes of consumers and between jurisdictions. In Victoria and New South Wales, contestability for larger consumers came into effect at a time of a comparative surplus of generation capacity and consequent low pool prices. However, in South Australia, the initial tranche of retail competition in July 2001 saw large increases in power bills for those involved. Given recent trends towards higher pool prices, the prospects are not encouraging for consumers when full retail competition is implemented in South Australia. It is interesting that both Queensland and the ACT have decided not to proceed down this path at this stage.

Conclusion

The immediate prospects for electricity consumers in South Australia appear bleak. Retail competition is scheduled to commence in 2003 at a time when there is little reserve capacity, and where existing capacity may be withdrawn at will or priced at extremely high levels. The pool-pricing mechanism is flawed and dangerously susceptible to manipulation. The ACCC in July 2002 refused to authorise changes to the market rules in the National Electricity Code which might have prohibited the more blatant bidding practices of generators. Competition from remote generators is limited by interconnection capacity and increases in that capacity are some years away. In any event, pool prices are equally open to manipulation in the other NEM regions. A fundamental rethink of the NEM design is likely to be required if consumers are to see any real long-term benefit, either in South Australia, or in the NEM as a whole.

CHAPTER 7

Energy and the Environmental Challenge

DENNIS MATTHEWS

The use of electricity has become so widespread that, along with transport fuel, it is generally regarded as a necessity alongside food, water, and shelter. Like transport fuel, the availability and price of electricity have become significant factors in our lives. Because electricity and transport fuel are inputs to many other products, they influence the price and availability of those products, creating a flow-on effect throughout the economy.

It is the services provided by electricity – hot water, light, heating, cooling, cooking etc. – that people desire. The same is true, in a much broader sense, for energy. We need a certain amount of energy in the form of food to keep us alive and to perform work. Energy is also needed for warmth and for growing the materials that we make into clothing. Many other uses of energy, however, are not so much needs as wants. These wants account for the majority of our energy use and are generally associated with a high standard of living. Energy drives the production of most of the goods and services that people in affluent countries like Australia take for granted.

Of all the produced forms of energy, electricity and transport fuels occupy special positions. These forms of energy have become so much a part of our lives that their availability and price play a dominant role in our lives. We see this during periods of fuel shortage or during power failures. The demand for transport fuel and electricity is so strong that, in times of short supply, people are prepared to pay significantly higher than normal prices. At the same time the availability and price of fuel and electricity are politically extremely contentious. Shortages and high prices for extended periods of time will not be suffered willingly without very good reason.

An electricity crisis

South Australians are facing an electricity crisis involving escalating electricity prices and possible power shortages. This constitutes an electricity crisis and the two problems are intimately related. The shortage of supply together with weak local competition, both within the electricity industry and from substitutes for electricity, have created a seller's market, leading to higher prices.

The crisis has been brought about by a number of factors. The Keating Government set up the National Electricity Market (NEM). The NEM brought with it the break-up and corporatisation of government-owned electricity utilities. For conservative, economic rationalist, pro-privatisation politicians this was a once-in-a-lifetime opportunity. Liberal governments in Victoria, and then in South Australia, quickly moved to exploit the opportunity by privatising their electricity assets. Attempts to privatise the electricity industry in NSW did not get the approval of the Labor Government.

Prior to the NEM and privatisation, the electricity industry was 'regulated' by the ballot box. Supply was kept ahead of demand and prices were kept low. To do otherwise was to court political disaster. After the NEM and privatisation, regulation became the province of politicians, who drew up acts of parliament, and of professional independent regulators, who were responsible for implementing these acts. Politicians now appear to be at arms' length, not only from the regulators and the electricity industry, but also from the political fallout that might ensue from the actions of the industry and its regulators. The NEM is however, a product of political choices, inspired by neo-liberal or economic rationalist political and economic ideology. The electricity market, the various acts, and the rules guiding the system are the result of these ideas.

Soon after the establishment of the NEM and the privatisation of the industry, wholesale prices started to rise dramatically. Just as fuel prices rise at times of high demand, such as long weekends and holidays, so electricity prices rise at times of high demand. As with transport fuel, there is no need for the electricity industry to collude, the increased demand is highly predictable, and windfall profits are there for the taking. The small numbers of suppliers of electricity during periods of high demand, such as during heat waves, exacerbate the problem. More companies are now moving into the lucrative area of peaking power stations. These are plants which operate at time of peak demand for power. The absence of comparable increases in baseload capacity means that those with peaking power stations can still demand prices 100 to 200 times the normal.

In the meantime, substitutes for electricity from fossil fuels have received almost no attention. Alternative measures such as energy conservation and efficiency measures, solar and wind electricity (both on- and off-grid) and solar heating have received little support either from government or industry. On the other hand, peaking power stations using polluting fuels have been given monopoly status.

These developments have occurred at a time when recognition of the harmful and costly effects of using fossil and nuclear fuels and the need for alternatives have gained greater prominence. More than ever, there is a need to implement a policy of environmentally friendly energy. Threats such as acid rain and smog and their accompanying impacts on health and the environment are now widely acknowledged. The world has now accepted the significant global threat posed by greenhouse gases emitted during the burning of fossil fuels.

With growing awareness of the necessity to develop environmentally friendly energy sources, some within the influential energy industry lobby are eager to see the development of nuclear power as the answer to Australia's sustainable energy needs.

Nuclear power
Events such as the nuclear meltdown at Three Mile Island in the US and the nuclear disaster at Chernobyl in the Ukraine have rightly been major setbacks for the nuclear power industry. Although nuclear power is stagnating, the industry still enjoys a high degree of government funding. The most recent example of this is the decommissioning of nuclear weapons, whereby large quantities of nuclear

fuel are released onto the market. This material, which was initially purchased by governments at very high prices, is now being sold at very low prices to the nuclear power industry.

Examples of government support for the nuclear industry in Australia include the funding of the nuclear science and engineering facility at Lucas Heights and the absence of stringent environmental controls on uranium mining, especially controls on underground acid leaching of uranium at Honeymoon and Beverley in South Australia. Government involvement in the nuclear power plant proposed for Jervis Bay in NSW is still being kept from public scrutiny, thirty years after the failed venture.

It should be remembered that South Australia has a long history of involvement in the nuclear industry – nuclear weapons testing for the British at Maralinga and Emu, mining uranium for nuclear weapons at Radium Hill, processing of the Radium Hill uranium at Port Pirie, testing of rockets to deliver nuclear weapons at Salisbury and Woomera, mining of uranium at Roxby Downs, Beverley and Honeymoon.

The electricity crisis in South Australia has implications for air pollution, greenhouse gas emissions, and nuclear fallout. We can go down the path of increased air pollution, greenhouse gas emission, and nuclear fallout or we can opt for a more benign approach which provides economic, social and environmental benefits through demand management and substitution.

Demand management and substitution

The demand for the services provided by energy may be met in a variety of ways. Cooking may be undertaken by electricity or gas. Hot water may be provided by electricity, gas or solar supply. Houses may be actively cooled using electric air conditioners or passively through house design, location, orientation and insulation. Transport may be provided using a variety of non-renewable fossil fuels, electricity from fossil fuels, gaseous and liquid fuels from renewable biomass and electricity from sunlight. It is important to note that, in a perfectly competitive market, all types of 'fuel' providing whichever service should be able to compete on equal terms; there should be no subsidies. Supply and demand will (in theory) lead to the best result for all concerned. There is, however, no such thing as perfect competition. Furthermore, not all costs are included in the supply–demand equation. Social, environmental and even economic costs are often omitted.

These anomalies are dealt with through a variety of mechanisms, including imposed regulations and subsidies. Subsidies and regulations which favour one type of service provider over another are anticompetitive. Subsidies may be justified in the name of competition; for example, by giving new and emerging technologies a leg up, or by assisting disadvantaged members of the society. All such subsidies should be transparent; there should be no hidden subsidies. Cross-subsidies, whereby one group of consumers subsidises another group, are anticompetitive.

As a result of the South Australian *Electricity Act 1996* and the associated South Australian *Independent Industry Regulator Act 1999* there are hidden subsidies to entrenched mature technologies and cross-subsidies between sections of the community. These subsidies disadvantage legitimate alternative service providers and are anticompetitive. Invariably the financially disadvantaged competitors are more environmentally benign than the areas that benefit from the subsidies.

In addition, the *Independent Industry Regulator Act* constrained the regulator to uniform statewide tariffs – the electricity tariff is the same irrespective of how far the electricity is transmitted, or how the distribution costs vary from locality to locality. Customers with low distribution costs subsidise those with high costs. This indirect subsidy discriminates against locally generated electricity and against alternative means of providing the same service; for example, gas for heating and cooking, solar for water heating, and solar electricity.

The formula for calculating the costs of increasing the capacity or upgrading the electricity distribution system (augmentation) is based on an assumed uniform growth in demand throughout South Australia. Customers in areas of low growth in demand subsidise those in areas of high growth. This is a hidden cross-subsidy, which subsidises augmentation of the electricity grid in areas of high demand and which discriminates against alternatives, including decreasing the demand for grid electricity. There is no rebate for consumers who decrease the demand for electricity from the grid and who delay costly upgrades (avoided augmentation). Decreasing the demand for grid electricity through energy-efficient buildings or by generating electricity onsite, goes unrewarded.

During the period in which these acts were being drawn up community consultation took place through a consumer consultative committee chaired by the 'Acting Independent Industry Regulator', Rob Lucas, who was the minister responsible for privatisation of the electricity industry in South Australia. In January 2000, a permanent appointment was made to the position of SA Independent Industry Regulator, the position title changing to Essential Services Commissioner under the incoming Labor Government in 2002.

Environmental, health and safety aspects of service provision are rarely included in the supply–demand equation. Even economic issues such as security of supply, local employment, and balance of payments are not included.

Existing power stations in South Australia have been given exemptions to air pollution legislation. In 2001 imported second-hand electricity generators were also given exemption from environmental legislation. Implementation of environmental standards costs money. However, the non-implementation of environmental standards costs money through damage to people's health and to the environment. Granting exemptions to these standards is a hidden subsidy that discriminates against less-polluting technology.

Environmentally compatible energy

South Australia has lagged behind the world and the rest of Australia in terms of promoting the use of energy in an environmentally compatible way. Housing in South Australia has become less and less energy-efficient over the last ten years. This has resulted in a surge in demand for large air conditioners and a corresponding increase in the summer peak electricity demand. This summer peak is responsible for the extremely high wholesale prices for electricity, which in turn have caused increases from 20–100% for all but the largest electricity consumers in South Australia. Large consumers, such as WMC's Olypmic Dam project at Roxby Downs, have been able to obtain price reductions, which means that other consumers must pay more.

Despite its favourable climate South Australia has one of the lowest per capita usages of solar hot water. About 3% of homes have solar hot water systems. In May 2001 the South Australian Government followed the lead of other states and introduced a solar hot water rebate, which, unfortunately is not available to businesses, to rental accommodation, or to public housing. Funding for the rebate is about $1million but the effect of this rebate on the contribution of solar to energy supplies in South Australia will be less than 0.1%.

Victoria introduced a solar hot water rebate in July 2000. The rebate was available for all residential, domestic, farm and community hot water use. Fifteen million dollars over three years were allocated for this purpose, where the individual rebate was $480 to $1500 (compared with $500 to $700 in South Australia).

The industry and employment benefits of a growing solar energy sector are substantial. Solar hot water systems are made entirely in Australia, replacing electricity from fossil-fuelled power stations which use imported equipment. Australia is a world leader in the development and manufacture of photovoltaic (solar cell) systems that replace either diesel fuel or electricity generated from fossil fuels and may be installed on roofs of buildings. More widespread use of this technology could reduce the threat of grid failure during peak summer demand.

Thanks to federal assistance there has been an upsurge in the use of photovoltaic cells for electricity generation in South Australia. Nevertheless, its contribution to electricity supply is still negligible and represents less than 0.5 megawatt (1000 kilowatts) of power, compared with 3500 megawatt generated by fossil fuel-based power stations.

South Australia is yet to take full advantage of the capacity of wind turbine electricity generation. There is currently only one medium-sized wind turbine in operation (based at Coober Pedy) although approval for additional turbines is expected over the next few years. Australia has very limited involvement in wind turbine manufacture although it does have a long history of experience with small wind turbines. Westwind in Western Australia manufactures larger machines which tend to be quieter and more cost-effective but they are also more obtrusive. The very large machines, which are likely to be adopted in the majority of wind farms in SA, are imported from countries like Denmark. South Australia has the potential to enter this industry through the expertise that exists at the Submarine Corporation.

The federal government's mandatory target for electricity generation from renewable energy is stimulating the development of wind farms for electricity generation. Once again, the target is such that electricity generated from wind energy will constitute less than 2% of all electricity used in South Australia.

In December 2001 the South Australian Government announced mandatory energy-efficiency standards for new buildings. Unfortunately the standards are set relatively low so the benefits will not be felt for many years.

Sustainable energy in SA

It is unlikely that any substantial momentum for the replacement of non-renewable fossil fuels will be generated *without* the establishment of a significant organisation devoted to the development and application of renewable energy alternatives. One exemplar worth examining is the Sustainable Energy Development Authority (SEDA) in NSW. It is emerging as a best-practice model and has been emulated by other states and territories but not yet by South Australia.

The NSW Government established SEDA in 1996, providing it with around $15 million per year to firmly establish it as a major player in the energy sector. In Victoria a Sustainable Energy Authority was set up to promote the development of sustainable energy options. The authority is supported by the Sustainable Energy Foundation designed to foster research and the uptake of environmentally sustainable energy. In 1999 the Queensland Office of Sustainable Energy was established, with a $35 million allocation from the state government over four years to promote energy efficiency and renewable energy. Western Australia has established the Australian Centre for Renewable Energy and the Sustainable Energy Authority.

In 1998 the South Australian Government lobbied the environment movement to support privatisation of the electricity industry. One of the inducements offered for its support was the establishment of a South Australian Sustainable Energy Authority. Multimillion-dollar funding for the authority was to come from electricity privatisation proceeds. A draft bill (*Sustainable Energy Bill*) for the authority was drawn up in 1998. The bill was supported by the Labor Opposition, the Democrats and independents Bob Such and Peter Lewis. The government hoped that the bill would persuade the Democrats to support privatisation. In the end they achieved this without the support of the Democrats, subsequently announcing in September 2001 that the state government would not proceed with the proposed Sustainable Energy Authority.

One reason for South Australia's lacklustre performance in this most important of energy sources is the lack of public and private funding being committed to research and development in the area. The State Energy Research Advisory Committee allocated just $0.14 million for this purpose over 2000–01.

In May 2001 the South Australian Liberal Government announced:

- a solar hot water rebate program (about $1 million)
- the establishment of the Sustainable Energy Advisory Committee
- increased funding for development and commercialisation of sustainable energy technologies and concepts (about $0.2 million per year)
- a sustainable energy awards program.

Neither the sustainable energy advisory committee nor the sustainable energy awards programs was initiated, and there has been no funding for sustainable energy projects in 2001–02.

The election of the Labor State Government in 2002 has seen some progress on these fronts. The new government has launched an energy-efficiency plan for the public sector, erected solar panels on the State Museum and appointed an officer to investigate the implementation of the recommendations of the Demand Side Taskforce established by the previous government. The Premier, Mike Rann, set an example on the solar energy front by installing a solar energy system on the roof of his house in Norwood soon after winning the state election. These are positive but modest early signs of progress.

Conclusion

Sustainable development is concerned with integrating economic, social and environmental objectives. In relation to electricity, this means having secure, accessible, affordable and clean ways of providing the services supplied by electricity. It makes little sense to burn limited, dirty fuels to boil water in order to generate electricity which is then used to heat water to 60°C. Yet this is what happens to about a third of the electricity used in our homes. By the time we use the hot water we have wasted over two-thirds of the energy in the fuel. Equipment is imported for generating the electricity and the profits from selling the electricity are exported.

In South Australia we should be maximising our use of solar energy to heat water. It makes no sense building poorly designed houses that require expensive, imported equipment to heat and cool them. Energy-efficient homes create local jobs. Poorly designed homes generate pollution and export jobs and profits overseas.

South Australia's electricity crisis will be ongoing unless action is taken to increase our energy efficiency and measures are taken to replace non-renewable electricity with renewable alternatives, such as solar hot water, wind turbines, and photovoltaic devices.

The triple bottom line from energy conservation and renewable energy is that it is cost-effective, socially desirable and environmentally benign. The transition to a socially, economically and environmentally sustainable energy industry in South Australia will require strategic and focussed leadership from the government, a leadership which recognises the importance of an energy policy for this state which is both far-sighted and innovative. A first significant display of leadership would most certainly be the establishment of an authority for sustainable energy.

Energy Efficiency, Equity and Sustainability

CHAPTER 8

Making Better Use of the Electricity We Have

Lessons from overseas

ANDREW NANCE

Introduction

South Australia's 'electricity crisis' is characterised as a problem of rising prices and inadequate supply. The debate focusses largely on options to increase supply, while largely ignoring the challenge of more efficiently using what we've already got.

The suite of alternative measures available to meet this challenge are called demand-side measures. This chapter argues that much more attention needs to be paid to the development and implementation of demand-side management (DSM) strategies. These include measures which aim to use less energy overall to achieve the same results (efficiency) and measures aimed at avoiding excessive peaks in demand (load shifting). The adoption of a DSM approach does not necessarily mean onerous regulations or supply restrictions. In fact, many effective measures continue to encourage 'choice' by having multiple markets but steer the markets towards more sustainable outcomes.

There are many good economic, environmental and social reasons to encourage energy efficiency. With Australia being one of the world leaders in per-capita energy consumption, there is a significant need to encourage more efficient use of energy.

The electricity price crisis facing South Australians in 2003 will inevitably generate considerable debate about how prices can be reduced. In this context DSM strategies offer the prospect of considerable price relief. This chapter outlines a range of DSM opportunities but with the caveat that not all strategies employed successfully elsewhere are readily transferable to South Australia due to the size and structure of our market and nature of our electricity load.

Restructuring and DSM

Although electricity industries are being 'restructured' around the globe, the general immaturity of reforms means that there are few, if any, direct parallels with the South Australian industry. Making international DSM comparisons is therefore fraught with danger – even drawing interstate comparisons is potentially flawed. The strategies reviewed in this chapter reflect this situation. They are derived from a report prepared by the International Energy Agency (IEA) which specifically identifies DSM practices that have proved to be effective in electricity industries being restructured.

So, what is 'restructuring'?

There are essentially four main aspects to the restructuring framework being adopted around the world (although the order and degree of implementation vary). These are:

- commercialisation, where commercial objectives are introduced into the management and operation of a state-owned (public) electricity business
- unbundling or disaggregation, where previously vertically integrated utilities (such as the old ETSA) are separated into legally and functionally distinct companies, each providing only one of the functions of generation, transmission, distribution and retailing
- privatisation, where publicly owned electricity sector assets pass into private ownership or control (SA and Victoria are the only Australian states to have privatised all assets)
- competition, which may be introduced into the system for selling electricity to the grid (wholesale competition which exists now) and providing electricity to end-use customers (retail competition which is being introduced progressively). The network services (transmission and distribution) of the industry are generally considered to be natural monopolies which are, as is the case in SA, regulated in the absence of competition.

The IEA acknowledges that incentives for DSM under commerciali-sation, disaggregation or privatisation can generally be maintained or strengthened through appropriate regulatory and government support. However, the introduction of competition provides much greater challenges due to the accompanying pressures for reduced government intervention. It is worth noting that very few, if any, examples of a functioning fully competitive electricity market exist worldwide – competition is generally quite limited everywhere, only the style and degree of regulation by government varies. Experience with the introduction of full retail contestability in Victoria is probably the most relevant example for analysts seeking to under-stand the likely impact of the introduction of retail competition in South Australia.

The South Australian electricity market

The National Electricity Market (NEM) comprises the states of Queensland, New South Wales (and the ACT), Victoria and South Australia. South Australia is joined to the interconnected 'national grid' by the Heywood interconnector in the south-east of the state. Depending on the context of the discussion, South Australia can be considered both a state and a 'region' or 'jurisdiction' in the NEM. Both state and federal governments are involved in shaping the market but state and territory governments have formal regulatory responsibility for the electricity industry.

Some of the international DSM practices discussed later in the chapter are better suited to implementation at a federal level although this would require the support of the states and territories.

Further interconnection of the South Australian transmission network has been approved, and the state will soon be directly con-nected to both New South Wales and Victoria. These and other developments will contribute to the further evolution of the NEM, creating a changing environment where policies and programs must keep pace. A number of the international DSM practices described here have been found to be effective, regardless of market structure and often even more so when introduced early in the change process – ideal for this current transition.

In considering the application of DSM strategies in South

Australia it should be acknowledged that a number of features of the industry in the state, when combined, make the South Australian market somewhat unique. One of the key features is the very hot summers. This has led to the proliferation of air conditioners in homes and offices. The SA Government Electricity Taskforce notes that the extensive use of air conditioning has resulted in South Australia having 'the most "peaky" demand of all NEM jurisdictions ... about 25% of installed capacity is required for only 5% of the time'.

The Electricity Supply Industry Planning Council (ESIPC) notes that:

In South Australia, the ratio of peak demand to average demand over summer is more than 2:1. The simple economic inefficiency of providing ever escalating capacity for short periods of demand must be addressed both inside the market place and, potentially, at a macro conservation policy level.

The 'peaks' in demand are probably the most notable feature of the SA market. They represent an obvious target for DSM strategies. Another feature of the South Australian industry requiring consideration is the 'size' of the market.

Compared to the other states participating in the NEM, SA comprises around 10% of the customers and consumes less than 8% of the total electric energy (NSW and ACT have 40% of the customers and 42% of the energy, Victoria 29% and 26%, Queensland 21% and 24%). Although the NEM is becoming more interconnected, the losses over these interconnectors (which impact on local costs) coupled with the nature of local fuel supplies (limited coal and natural gas) means that the SA region of the NEM will continue to behave differently from the rest of the market.

Just how much competition can exist in a (sub) market of this size is the subject of considerable speculation, but many of the DSM practices discussed here rely on a healthy level of competition for energy products and services. Their effectiveness may be limited by the level of competition that can be sustained, particularly in the residential sector. It appears likely that only one other operator will attempt to compete with the incumbent franchise retailer, AGL SA. If this prevails, continued regulatory oversight will be required and those in public office will find themselves under extreme pressure from a range of stakeholders.

The performance of the state economy also exerts significant influence on the demand for electricity. Higher economic, employment and population growth rates generally increase the demand for electricity. South Australia's relatively low rates of growth mean that growth in demand for electricity is lower relative to the eastern states.

There are, of course, many more issues that distinguish SA in the electricity markets, including community attitudes and social standards. All of these factors should be kept in mind when looking for uniquely South Australian solutions to the quest for a sustainable energy future.

The IEA and DSM

The IEA is an autonomous agency within the framework of the Organisation for Economic Co-operation and Development (OECD). It was established in 1974 to facilitate cooperation amongst its member countries on energy issues, particularly those relating to market-based reforms.

The IEA DSM program is a relatively new collaboration, commencing in 1993. It aims to identify and promote opportunities for DSM. The program is divided into a number of 'tasks' each involving significant research. The report discussed here was released in late 2000 and titled *Mechanisms for Promoting DSM and Energy Efficiency in Changing Electricity Businesses*. The objective of the research underpinning this report was to:

... develop in detail a range of practical mechanisms for promoting the implementation of economically justifiable DSM in changing electricity businesses, such as in restructured electricity industries and competitive electricity markets.

Interestingly, Australia provided many of the drivers of this research, with the motivation for the study coming from Australia's preparations for the NEM.

The report identifies and discusses 25 mechanisms in some depth. These are presented in the four broad categories of control, support, funding and market (see appendix). It should be noted that these categories áre intended to operate as part of a multi-faceted strategy with appropriate elements drawn from each category. The categories provide an integrated framework to assist with the evaluation of DSM programs. A weakness in any one category is likely to dramatically reduce the effectiveness of the overall package. The significance of each of these categories is briefly explained below.

A strong *control* category is required in effective DSM programs. Regulation and intervention are necessary to compensate for any market failures. The immaturity of the market, absence of competition and the necessity for consumer protection means control will need to be exercised for the foreseeable future.

The *support* category refers to ensuring that issues such as information, training, advice, a services market with trained practitioners and so on are provided.

The *funding* category refers to financial 'carrots and sticks' used to promote DSM, while the *market* category refers to the many market-based activities which, with appropriate government encouragement and incentives and industry support, can deliver a demand-based response to a market otherwise totally dominated by supply-side influences.

Control mechanisms

This category groups together mechanisms that compel market participants to achieve efficiency targets and/or employ specific techniques and strategies in their operations. Such command-and-control policy measures are historically unpopular with industry which often opposes interventionist government actions. Typically mechanisms such as these must be accompanied by a regulatory or policing regime that can sometimes prove cumbersome and expensive.

However, if levels of competition in the market are failing to bring results through market-based strategies such as those discussed later, government intervention through mechanisms in the control category are an important alternative.

The IEA lists five mechanisms in this category. Two of these represent quite broad 'approaches' to regulation. *Integrated resource planning* (IRP) is an elegant methodology that, unfortunately, is most effective in vertically integrated monopoly electricity businesses like the formerly publicly owned ETSA. The aim of IRP is to determine the lowest cost option for meeting a consumer's energy needs. This is achieved by consideration of both supply-side and demand-side options and the consideration of environmental and social costs whenever possible. The disaggregation of the industry and the narrow commercial imperatives of the resultant market participants have removed incentives (for generators and retailers at least) to employ IRP principles.

Revenue regulation is another elegant methodology and one which operates on a very important principle, that of decoupling sales volume from revenue. (For example, an electricity retailer could increase profits without encouraging its customers to consume more energy. In fact they could increase profits by encouraging their customers to use less!) Under this mechanism the total allowable revenue of an electricity business is set at a particular dollar figure. Within this cap, the business is free to set its own price structure and any over- or under-collection of revenue is balanced the following year. This has been employed to varying degrees in Australia to network businesses and retail franchise businesses although not always with the specific intention of improving energy efficiency.

In principle, revenue regulation is regarded as a 'light handed and low cost' form of regulation that is still applicable to the monopoly elements of the industry and is acceptable under the National Electricity Code. In South Australia, the electricity pricing order (EPO) currently applies to the market's transmission, distribution and retail participants. While the EPO provides for some revenue regulation for prescribed transmission and distribution services, in relation to retail it only applies to the tariffs that may be charged.

The decoupling of profit from sales volume encourages retailers to see themselves as providers of hot water, climate control, cooking heat, light and power rather than merely providers of kilowatt hours and consequently is seen as a positive driver of energy efficiency. This represents a significant change in approach to energy supply and use that should not be lost in the political quest for 'cheaper electricity for all'. Revenue regulation is not seen as appropriate for retailers under full contestability conditions but, should healthy levels of competition fail to appear, it could be reinstated as a viable retail regulation option.

This leads on to a mechanism which is well suited to the South Australian situation – *energy-efficiency license conditions for electricity businesses*, an instrument for delivery rather than a strategy for efficiency gains themselves. The licensing of electricity businesses falls within the jurisdiction of the South Australian Independent Industry Regulator and compliance processes already exist. Presently, the retail code policed by the South Australian industry regulator contains a brief set of requirements to enable retailers to provide advice to residential customers on how to reduce electricity costs, how to arrange an energy audit and typical running costs of major appliances. The aim would be to expand these licence conditions to mandate defined DSM outcomes in all sectors of the market – from generation to transmission to distribution to retailing.

Overall, control mechanism opportunities in SA include expansion of the retailers' advice requirements, supporting national initiatives to enforce efficiency standards and ensuring that DSM initiatives have the opportunity to compete with supply options in a holistic planning process for the physical electricity network. For such mechanisms to be effective however, an agreed methodology for the quantification of energy savings and for ensuring compliance must be developed. It should also be noted that other mechanisms, such as those discussed below, would need to be established to provide the capability for market participants to deliver mandated savings.

Funding mechanisms

Many of the mechanisms and programs (such as energy-efficiency information, education, training and demonstration programs) identified by the IEA require some sort of upfront and/or continued funding. This report only identifies two main funding streams – extracting money through some sort of transaction cost in the market's day-to-day operation or requiring electricity business to pay.

A *public benefits charge for energy efficiency*, is sometimes referred to as a 'system benefits' or 'wires' charge or a 'non-bypassable' levy and is a method for raising funds from the operation of the market. In this report the IEA recommends a small charge on the transmission/distribution businesses as being the least politically offensive fundraising option. This is also independent of the remaining stages of market restructuring and thus is appropriate for South Australia.

Electricity retailers can play a role in bundling financing and energy-efficiency services for customers and the new business opportunities such a service may create. This practice already takes place to a certain extent in SA, although almost exclusively with consumers from the 'big end of town'. Opportunities at the household level could be as simple as financing an efficient fridge at low or no interest, or the provision of leasing arrangements. Questions on how the retailer would raise sufficient capital to ensure the widespread impact of these measures need to be addressed, and ultimately, uptake is dependent on the commercial attitude of the retailer, and while this can be encouraged, it cannot be mandated. It does, however, offer enormous potential for positive social and environmental outcomes.

Other proposed funding alternatives include revenue generated by a national carbon tax scheme or other schemes following the 'polluter pays' principle. Regardless of how the funds are generated, a rotating pool of funds can be established – topped up by the energy savings achieved.

It should be noted that at least some of this cost will inevitably flow to consumers. It is therefore imperative that programs funded in this way are diverse (to service as many of the contributors as possible), yet strategically targetted to yield efficiency gains for all consumers.

Support mechanisms

This category deals with the non-financial resources required to support the more efficient use of energy. This includes schemes that encourage the training of practitioners and the growth of businesses which provide energy-efficiency services. These mechanisms typically see governments developing partnerships with the business sector, thereby spreading costs, providing employment opportunities and delivering greater resources than governments could hope to achieve on their own.

Building a network of informed *allies* is one category of support mechanisms. Industry associations, tradespeople, appliance and equipment retailers either make energy decisions or can influence the decision-makers by providing efficiency information. Significant opportunities exist in SA to structure training programs aimed at these people.

The establishment of *energy centres*, organisations whose sole aim is to advocate energy efficiency and DSM, offers yet another example in this category. Some degree of public funding will be required if it is assumed that electricity businesses would not be commercially motivated to establish such organisations themselves. Such centres could operate on a similar model to that of Adelaide's Home Ideas Centre – as a permanent working expo, or be incorporated into energy-efficient demonstration homes. Other services such as training workshops, home energy audits and so on, could also be incorporated and strong links to community groups established and developed.

In 1998 a bill to establish a Sustainable Energy Authority was introduced into the South Australian Parliament as part of the suite of legislation surrounding the sale of ETSA. Despite receiving strong support from the two main opposition parties and key Independents, the bill was allowed to lapse. The creation of this organisation would have implemented the IEA's *creating entrepreneurial energy organisations* mechanism, whereby an organisation is mandated to achieve defined energy-efficiency outcomes. These are distinguished from the energy centres described above by being much more commercially oriented and often, with the eventual aim of being self-funding. NSW's Sustainable Energy Development Authority (SEDA) is held up as a successful example of such an organisation.

Considered by the IEA to be most effective under competition, such an organisation can be an important link between consumers, community groups, energy services companies, industry and training providers, one which identifies opportunities for transforming the market in areas such as the commercialisation and mainstreaming of technologies and practices. Increasingly popular with governments worldwide, the potential for such an organisation in South Australia is limited by the size of the market here and may be more viable as an extension of the energy centre concept rather than as a separate organisation.

Aggregating electricity purchases is another component of the support mechanism category designed to achieve energy efficiency, and encompasses the potential for customers to influence retailers through purchasing power in a competitive market. Efficiency outcomes are typically obtained by bundling other services into the purchasing agreement – such as a specific 'green power' component, energy audits or similar. This mechanism represents an enormous opportunity applicable only under contestable retail conditions and allows competing retailers to further distinguish themselves and establish a unique relationship with their customers. Four Victorian city councils have established a 'community power' body and are pursuing aggregated purchases in Victoria's newly contestable retail market.

In the South Australian context, it is crucial that the government commits to ambitious but achievable targets for renewable energy and energy-efficiency services in its own aggregated electricity purchases and ensures that the regulatory framework has been established for other groups to pursue aggregated purchases for possible efficiency gains. Social welfare concerns may in part be addressed through this mechanism, an example being aggregated purchasing for tenants of South Australian Housing Trust properties.

Overall, there are many opportunities in SA to enhance this broad category of support for energy efficiency. One of the prime issues is the need to establish an independent organisation or organisations to coordinate and deliver many of these support services and programs. Energy SA currently performs a similar role along with its many other responsibilities in the energy sector. However, a number of questions are relevant here. Can Energy SA provide the necessary independence? Can Energy SA or another government agency accommodate the entrepreneurial, commercial and financial activities described above? Can funding be secured for alternative organisations? Can duplication of federal and other state-based activities be avoided? These and other questions would require satisfactory answers before advocating an expansion of Energy SA's role to include the creation of a South Australian equivalent of SEDA.

Market mechanisms

This category groups together 11 mechanisms to guide market forces toward delivering energy-efficient behaviour. In essence, the mechanisms look at the role of taxation, price signals, 'brand' marketing, aggregated purchases and load curtailment in delivering demand-side responses.

One strategy whereby energy is taxed is based on the premise that increased energy prices will result in increased efficiency and represents more of a federal opportunity, probably as part of the National Greenhouse Strategy. An energy tax is similar to a carbon tax except that is does not discriminate against fossil fuels. By way of example, The Netherlands levies a tax based equally on energy and carbon content; Denmark also levies a carbon dioxide and energy tax, but relief can be obtained by committing to energy-efficiency programs. Likewise, in the UK, relief is given to high-energy users exposed to international competition by lowering the levy if they agree to efficiency targets. The UK system also aims for overall tax neutrality by cutting other business taxes and many Australian advocates see this as an important offset if such a tax were to be applied.

There is increasing recognition that, for the residential sector at least, electricity price rises do not necessarily lead to reduced demand. Broad application of such a tax may therefore not only be politically unpopular, but of questionable effectiveness as a direct promoter of home-energy efficiency. There does appear, however, to be increasing government implementation of similar taxes acting as a source of funding rather than as a trigger of behavioural change in itself.

Tax exemptions and incentives for energy efficiency offer another example of a market mechanism and typically involve a reduction in tax liability to those who either invest in or carry out activities aimed at achieving energy savings. The mechanism is normally directed at industrial and commercial consumers through schemes such as favourable depreciation rates, reduced GST or other taxes for energy-efficient equipment. Although most taxation issues must be tackled at the federal level, there are still opportunities for South

Australia to exercise influence within the state's taxation scope. Some believe that such a mechanism has the added benefit of directly attracting the interest of company financial controllers, not just engineers and facility managers.

As mentioned in the introduction, intra-state competition to attract employment-generating investment often sees state governments granting tax concessions to investors. An opportunity therefore exists to link this 'favourable' treatment to a commitment to an energy-efficiency program.

Ensuring that electricity markets provide appropriate signals to encourage, rather than discourage energy efficiency is included in this category. The IEA report strongly advocates enhanced communication between retailer and customer through a number of avenues: real-time communication with customers engaged on a curtailment agreement (large loads are switched off when demand and pool prices are high), time-of-use and peak-demand tariff structures for customers with suitable metering or improved billing information and more frequent billing cycles.

Contestable customers already have peak demand-based, time-of-use tariffs available for their network charges. Although existing customers cannot be forced to adopt such tariffs, this practice is being actively encouraged in the market. The South Australian industry regulator's retail code also specifies quite comprehensive information required in any retailer's bill but this becomes even more relevant under competition and the minimum standards must be continually revised as the market develops.

These *communication* mechanisms are certainly viewed as effective for reducing peak loads – extremely relevant in SA – but rely on customers not only being aware of price signals sent by the market (via the retailer) but also being willing and able to do something about them. The mechanisms are therefore, at best, a component of a much broader strategy. Relevant to this is the current debate around electricity meter alternatives for soon-to-be-contestable consumers (residential and small business). The type of electricity meters used can greatly enhance DSM effects but the adoption of these is not a cure-all and should be remembered when debating the expenditure required for implementation to all customers.

The marketing techniques described in the IEA report include *energy performance labelling* and *developing an energy-efficient brand*. Labelling describes initiatives to better inform consumers about the likely energy performance of their purchases. Two basic types of ratings are described by the IEA: 'endorsement' labels such as the 'energy star' label for appliances meeting prescribed energy performance while in stand-by, and 'comparison' labels such as the 0–6 star labels for white goods. While Australia has a quite well-developed program for 'rating' appliances, cars and houses, most opportunities for further effect lie in mandating minimum standards and in better education of consumers and point-of-sale representatives (appliance retailers, tradespeople) on accurate interpretation and comparison of the ratings, a role for the 'support' mechanisms discussed earlier. It is also important for government purchasing guidelines to show leadership and exploit market power by reflecting the life cycle cost advantages of energy-efficient purchases.

SA introduced minimum residential building energy performance standards in 2002. Opportunities obviously exist to raise these over time, but more important may be the extension of these to the rental sector. Mandating the raising of an energy performance certificate for properties prior to tenancy (or sale), as is the case in the ACT, has the potential to overcome a major barrier to efficiency investments in rented properties – the 'split incentive' between property owner and tenant (as identified in a recent Productivity Commission report). Such a requirement would need phasing in to allow for some growth in supporting infrastructure (energy-rating assessors and retro-fitters for example), but is a conceivable near-term goal that could yield significant gains in the energy performance of existing housing stock.

The use of branding as a marketing tool for energy efficiency is a concept even more relevant in competitive electricity markets. The national trademark, 'GreenPower', the renewable energy accreditation scheme and SEDA's 'Energy Smart' programs are examples of successful implementation of this strategy. Branding can be applied to a myriad of activities but success lies in a credible accreditation process, although this does not necessarily mean a government accrediting agency. Opportunities exist for a state-level branding scheme in SA which would rely on a network of trade allies to deliver a range of energy-efficiency and renewable energy-related services. Plumbers, electricians, home maintenance franchise operators, appliance retailers and other trade allies who have completed a training and accreditation scheme relevant to their field could be endorsed as 'energy partners'.

The remaining mechanisms outlined in the report focus on the provision of energy services.

Energy performance contracting is a well-established practice in Europe and the US and involves an 'energy service company' (ESCO) identifying, implementing and guaranteeing energy-efficiency improvements in an organisation and being paid from a negotiated proportion of the cost reductions derived from the energy savings. Services may include project management and training. The energy savings would also be used to fund the capital investment required, often through a financing arrangement established with the ESCO, a third party or even an electricity retailing business. The Australian Energy Performance Contracting Association (AEPCA) represents many organisations which fall into the ESCO category and has developed national guidelines and benchmarks in conjunction with the Australian Greenhouse Office (AGO). The AEPCA is an active and rapidly evolving organisation but active participation and promotion by government certainly has scope for growth in SA.

The existence of an 'energy services' market means that competition can and should exist for these services. Ideally this would lead to greater innovation and increased standards. In this context, competitive sourcing of energy services describes an opportunity for large energy users (or an aggregation of smaller users) to specify their energy requirements to multiple electricity retailers and/or ESCOs whose responses are assessed in a competitive tender process. Examples of such a strategy may include:

- a paper mill considering cogeneration (of electricity and process heat or steam)
- a local government acting as an electricity aggregator
- a hospital seeking to enhance efficiency and reliability
- a chain of retail stores seeking reduced electricity costs and enhanced public image.

This 'services' market can be expanded to include larger-scale DSM requirements which can be specified in a public tender process. This is seen as a market-based way for network businesses and retailers to fulfill obligations imposed on them under some of the control mechanisms, such as energy-efficiency license conditions, discussed earlier. The tender responses are assessed competitively, with the successful tenderer(s) engaged commercially to deliver their promises. Tenderers could be large energy users, ESCOs or even energy centres or entrepreneurial energy organisations (such as SEDA). This could also see supply-side and demand-side solutions to network limitations competing transparently and adhering to the integrated resource planning methodology discussed earlier. (Imagine a substation upgrade becoming irrelevant because consumers have installed solar water heaters and roof insulation and planted shade trees!)

These services market mechanisms are rated highly by the IEA for use in competitive energy markets as they bring together many of the other mechanism categories. Success relies heavily on the level of competition that can be established in the market but represents a significant opportunity to exploit the so-called benefits of restructuring. Success in a market the size of South Australia is quite possible and a role exists for government to encourage and facilitate these mechanisms as a demonstration of the benefits available from increased competition. This also represents a long-term employment opportunity and should be regarded as essential in the economic development of this state.

Demand-side bidding

Wholesale trading in the NEM is essentially a supply-only market. Demand-side bidding, or DSB schemes provide for load-reduction capacity to compete with generation capacity in the wholesale electricity pool. Customers would bid a price level above which they would reduce demand into the wholesale pool. The only expected DSM outcome is load shifting (peak reduction) but this is very desirable in the SA context. This mechanism has been explored to some degree already in the NEM but participation has been poor. Many large energy users do not see this as something they can participate in as it requires an ability to 'shut-down' part of their operations at short notice. As a result, estimates of the impact of voluntary load curtailment on summer peaks are, at best, in the order of single-digit percentages.

Conclusion

This chapter has attempted to highlight the potential effectiveness of DSM principles and strategies. It appears that many opportunities exist within the SA market for the application of these. However, within the evolution of the market it must be recognised that a limited amount of competition (in generation and retail especially) is likely to exist in this, the smallest region of the NEM.

Widespread, effective DSM does appear to rely on an active 'energy services' market and increasing activities in the 'support' category. The obvious employment opportunities this market has the potential to create are equal to those in manufacturing, sales and services. These 'sustainable energy' jobs should be a target of economic development policy, exploiting the fact that sustainable energy *can* deliver benefits to the economy, the environment and most importantly – to society.

The state government and its agencies have broad responsibilities as leaders and facilitators of energy-efficiency programs – all of which are vital to the establishment of a culture of 'energy efficiency'. This chapter has attempted to provide some ideas to help inspire the realisation of this objective.

References

ESIPC (Electricity Supply Industry Planning Council) 2001, *Annual planning review*, ESIPC, Adelaide.

IEA (International Energy Agency), Demand-Side Management Programme 2000, *Developing mechanisms for promoting demand-side management and energy efficiency in changing electricity businesses, research report no. 3, task VI*, available at www.dsm.iea.org

Appendix: IEA-developed DSM mechanisms

Control mechanisms: energy businesses are directed to change behaviour through legislation and regulation
Mandatory sourcing of energy efficiency
Energy-efficiency licence conditions for electricity businesses
Integrated resource planning (IRP)
DSM and energy efficiency as alternatives to network expansion
Revenue regulation
Funding mechanisms: provide funding for other mechanisms
Public benefits' charge for energy efficiency
Financing of energy efficiency by electricity businesses
Support mechanisms: provide support for behavioural changes by both end-users and energy businesses
Sustainable energy training schemes for practitioners
Energy centres
Creating entrepreneurial energy organisations
Developing the energy-service company (ESCO) industry
Promotion of energy efficiency by industry associations
Aggregating electricity purchases to achieve energy efficiency
Voluntary agreements for energy efficiency
Market mechanisms: market forces are used to encourage behavioural changes by end-users and electricity businesses
Taxes on energy
Tax exemptions and incentives for energy efficiency
Providing consumption information on customer's electricity bills
Communicating pricing and other information for energy efficiency
Energy performance labelling
Developing an energy-efficient brand
Cooperative procurement of energy-efficient appliances and equipment
Energy performance contracting
Competitive sourcing of energy services
Competitive sourcing of demand-side resources
Demand-side bidding in competitive markets.

CHAPTER 9

How Can We Use Electricity More Efficiently?

JOHN DENLAY

Introduction

South Australia is in the midst of an electricity crisis. In the last two years, media reports of summer blackouts, supply shortages and rising electricity prices have become commonplace.

To date the state government's response has been to promote the building of more oil/gas-fired local power stations. Additional connectors to coal-fired power stations in NSW and Victoria have also been promoted. All of these mean even more reliance on fossil fuels such as coal, oil and natural gas.

Increased fossil fuel reliance also means increased greenhouse gas emissions. Scientists internationally, including those at the Commonwealth Scientific and Industrial Research Organisation (CSIRO), are predicting significant changes to the planet's climates as a result of the emissions of greenhouse gases.

However, the current shortage of supply (or put another way, excess of demand) presents an opportunity to reduce demand and substitute supply with renewable sources in cost-effective ways, at the same time as making a positive contribution to curbing the growth of greenhouse gas emissions.

Demand-side management turns the tables on a supply-focussed electricity industry. Rather than continually expanding the supply system to meet every growing demand, energy efficiency and load management are used as tools to contain, and ideally reduce energy use.

Current problems with electricity in SA

The South Australian Government's Electricity Supply Industry Planning Council (ESIPC) is projecting significant increases in the supply of electricity from fossil fuels (ESIPC 2000).

The main responses to this rising peak electricity demand has been to commission further fossil fuel-powered peaking plants, to upgrade the distribution system and to propose additional electricity interconnectors which enable the importation of electricity from other states. Such 'supply-side' approaches will see even greater greenhouse emissions, as demand remains unchecked and more polluting electricity is imported from NSW and Victoria.

How these problems impact on the environment

According to the National Greenhouse Gas Inventory conducted by the Australian Greenhouse Office (AGO) in 1998, producing electricity from fossil fuels is the single largest source of greenhouse gas emissions in Australia (37% of total CO_2-equivalent emissions in 1998).

At the same time, CSIRO scientists have indicated that projected emissions of greenhouse gases are likely to result in the following climate changes in Adelaide:

- increased temperatures with around 1° to 5°C increase in temperature are predicted.
- more extreme hot days are predicted with the number of days above 35°C expected to increase from the current average of 10 days per year to somewhere between 13 and 28 days per year by 2070.
- less rainfall and more evaporation are predicted, with the likely scenario being less rainfall in Adelaide. Models predict a change of rainfall between +10% and −35% by 2070. Even if rainfall does increase, higher evaporation rates, produced by increased temperatures will mean that, in all scenarios, there will be a net water balance deficit.

Climate impacts are likely even if greenhouse gas emissions are curtailed. The lower end of these impacts rely on stabilising CO_2 concentrations in the atmosphere to 1990 levels 'within a few decades' and 'eventually CO_2 emissions would need to decline to a very small fraction of current emissions' (IPCC 2001, p. 7).

The insidious nature of climate change means that increasing temperatures may well place greater demand on peak electricity demand through, for example, increasing use of air conditioning – driving further increases in greenhouse gas emissions.

Reducing energy use

Australians' wasteful use of energy is a major contributor to our unenviable record of being the world's highest per-capita emitters of greenhouse gases. Of course most people don't waste energy for the sake of it; rather, the availability of relatively cheap electricity and few controls on its use have seen the emergence of highly inefficient appliances and scant consideration for passive heating and cooling in homes.

For most households, the largest energy user is the electric water heater. (However, householders may not be aware of this, as the electricity for off-peak water heaters is only one-third of the price of peak electricity.) According to Energy SA, an off-peak electric water heater can be responsible for 4.7 tonnes of greenhouse gas emissions per year, where a comparable electric-booster solar water heater only contributes 1.4 tonnes. Given that a typical household is responsible for around 15 tonnes of greenhouse gas emissions per year, the 3.3 tonne difference is quite significant.

Switching from electric to solar water heating is an example of reducing energy use through more efficient technology. The AGO has demonstrated that energy can also be conserved through changes in behaviour; for example, raising the thermostat on an air conditioner by 1°C (that is, from 24° to 25°C) can reduce energy use by 10%. And washing clothes in cold water uses only one-fifth of the energy of a hot wash.

Peak demand management

Clearly one of the challenges facing policy-makers is to develop effective electricity demand management strategies to counter the negative environmental, social and economic consequences of excessive use. In addition to using electricity more efficiently, the end-users of electricity can also play a role in modifying the timing of electricity use.

The ways in which peak demand can be managed include interrupting and rescheduling non-essential loads using local stand-by generators during peak periods, incorporating ice storage into air conditioning systems (so they operate during off-peak periods) and correcting power-factor* for industries with highly inductive loads.

The way in which peak loads are managed – through off-peak tariffs for uses such as water heating – offers a good example of how load management can lead to energy inefficiency. The lower off-peak tariffs encourage the use of water heating – a highly inefficient form, with storage losses from tank and pipes of around 30%.

There are numerous ways in which peak demand can be reduced energy-efficiently; for example, turning off second fridges and freezers in households not only reduces demand during hot days, when the appliances are working hardest, but also reduces energy throughout the year.

Embedded generation

Not only has the electricity industry been supply-focussed, it has also given most attention to the distribution of electricity produced from large centralised power stations. Opportunities for more decentralised supply, such as roof-top photovoltaics, local windpower and cogeneration, have not received the attention they deserve.

While all of these 'supply' electricity, they do have a role in demand-side management as they can sit within a local distribution network, reducing the demand placed on distant generators and transmission systems. For this reason they are often termed 'embedded generation'. Indeed, there can often be blurring of distinctions between local generation and energy efficiency. For example, is a solar water heater an energy-efficient product or a local energy generator?

---

* Power factor is a measure of how much of the transmitted electrical energy ends up doing useful work. In loads such as motors, some of the electrical energy is used to sustain the motor's magnetic fields. The total 'apparent' energy delivered is measured in VoltAmps (VA), while the energy that does actual work is measured in Watts (W). An electrical system with a poor power factor will need greater generation and network capacity to deliver the same amount of work as will one with a good power factor.

Residential sector demand-side management

The residential sector accounts for around one-third of electricity use in SA and is a major contributor to the rapid growth in peak demand. The growth in sales in residential air conditioning is widely regarded as being a major contributor to this demand.

ETSA Utilities claims that approximately 65,000 air conditioners are sold in SA each year, many of which are likely to be upgrades from window boxes to higher-powered units such as split and ducted reverse-cycle air conditioners.

To meet this growth in air-conditioner installation, two new peaking power plants were installed in 2001 at a cost of around $90–100 million each. According to Origin Energy (2001):

The combined effect of reverse cycle and refrigerative air-conditioning uptake and the requirement for installation of peaking generation capacity means that there is approximately $400–500 million a year being spent on keeping cool for those few short hot days of summer. This is not a sustainable outcome for a state of 1.5 million people.

These air conditioners are being used in houses which have been built with no requirements for shading or insulation. An Australian Bureau of Statistics (ABS) study records that 29.2% of SA households are not insulated.

Of course, air conditioners are not the only appliances used by households during periods of peak demands. Again, according to the ABS, 99.9% of SA homes have at least one refrigerator and 27.2% have two or more. Almost half (47.4%) of these refrigerators are 10 or more years old. Other loads likely to be important include separate freezers (42.8% of SA homes have one or more), pool pumps and other household appliances.

Main contributors to energy use

A convenient means of quantifying the main components of residential energy use is through the identification of each component's contribution to greenhouse gas emissions.

Of a typical Australian household's 15 tonnes of greenhouse gas emissions, around 56% is the result of energy use. Based on 1999 information from Energy SA this energy use is made up of:

- water heating – 29%
- space heating and cooling – 11%
- fridges and freezers – 18%
- other appliances – 20%
- standby power – 8%
- lighting – 9%
- cooking – 5%.

While the list includes energy produced from all sources, including electricity, gas and wood, many of the significant categories such as fridges and freezers, appliances, standby power and lighting would be exclusively powered by electricity. Also according to the ABS, 50.8% of SA homes use electricity for water heating, 51.8% use it for cooking, and 38.4% use it for cooling.

Opportunities

The table on pages 144–5 presents a range of opportunities for managing demand in the residential sector. Each option is presented with an assessment of how effective it would be in reducing peak demand and general energy use.

The realisation of these initiatives will require involvement from government, industry and householders. An overview of the roles these different groups can play in fostering energy efficiency in South Australia is provided below.

Roles for households

- participate in community workshops on energy efficiency
- take part in home energy audit and retrofitting programs
- respond to price signals and other incentives
- take action to reduce electricity use

How to foster this action:

- state and local government and community groups to provide community education, audits and retrofit programs
- involvement in Cool Communities projects

- Energy SA and TAFE to develop education curriculum and training accreditation to support education, audit and retrofit programs
- retailers to provide financing for efficiency purchases, tariffs to encourage conservation and information on billing to feedback progress

Roles for electricity retailers
- shift from selling electricity to selling energy-related services
- loans to customers for energy-efficient products and services
- provision for repayment of loans through electricity bills. Importantly, this can allow tenants the same opportunities for energy efficiency as homeowners
- provision of greenhouse gas emission information on electricity bills, with households benchmarked against 'green' homes

How to foster this action:
- EPA to set greenhouse gas emission reduction targets for retailers to foster their provision of energy services
- the Essential Services Commission (ESCOSA) to require, through licences, the inclusion of greenhouse information on electricity bills

An excellent model of electricity retailer involvement is the Sacramento Municipal Utility District (www.smud.org). Features of this district's energy service activities include:

- $US50 incentive to turn in 'spare' (typically inefficient) refrigerators
- rebates for efficient air conditioning, refrigeration, clothes washers, insulation, and shading
- $US750 rebate and 10-year, low-interest loan for solar water heaters. This service also includes free 5- and 10-year maintenance inspections
- 100% financing for up to 10 years for installing efficient windows
- coupons for $US4 off compact fluorescents
- free shade trees

Use	Ways of reducing	Effectiveness:		Notes
		Peak demand	Energy use	
Water heating	Convert to AAA rated shower heads and aerators	Limited (instant electric units)	Very good	Showerheads can save $50–100 annually of combined elec. and water bills. 90% of homes don't have them.
	Solar water heater	Limited	Very good	With rebates & Renewable Energy Certificates, payback is less than warranty period. Upfront cost a major barrier. Potential cost reduction with expanded local industry.
	Improved efficiency of existing electric water heaters	Limited	Very good	Many thermostats set to 75°C. Few units have blanket insulation.
	Behaviour: cold water clothes washing, shorter showers	Limited	Very good	47% of households wash clothes in hot water.
Heating and cooling	Insulation	Very good	Good	35% of homes don't have ceiling insulation. Good potential to improve home comfort.
	Shading and draft proofing	Very good	Good	Shading significant for peak summer demand.
	Zoning (i.e. only heating/cooling room used)	Very good	Good	Education to encourage zoning in existing homes and standards for new homes.
	Turning thermostat: up (summer); down (winter)	Very good	Good	Each degree of thermostat change can reduce energy use by 10%.

Use	Ways of reducing	Effectiveness:		Notes
		Peak demand	Energy use	
	More efficient active heating and cooling systems i.e. evaporative cooling	Very good relative to ducted R/C	Good	Evaporative coolers good compared to ducted reverse cycle. Need to compare how a ducted evap system compares with a split R/C aircon.
	Single room R/C rather than ducted	Very good relative to ducted	Good	Good compared to ducted R/C. But new units do add peak load.
Fridges and freezers	Turning off 2nd fridge/ freezer	Very good	Very good	$120 saving per year. Significant benefit to peak load.
	Upgrading to 5-star fridge/freezer	Very good	Very good	Many efficient appliances can be cost-competitive.
	Behaviour: avoiding regular opening of fridge)	Good	Good	How a household uses their fridge can significantly impact on demand/ energy use.
Lighting	Convert to compact fluorescents	Moderate	Good	Scope for $70 savings over life of globe.
	Behaviour: turning off lights	Moderate	Good	Highly visible form of energy wastage.
Appliances	Behaviour: turning off (not just standby)	Good	Good	Households can spend $95/yr on standby.
	Behaviour: using appliance outside peak times	Good	No benefit	Shifting appliance use to non-peak times reduces peak demand, but not energy use.
	More efficient appliances	Good	Good	Many efficient appliances can be cost-competitive.

Roles for plumbers and electricians
- key providers of energy-efficiency advice, services and products (especially solar water heaters and AAA-rated showerheads and aerators) to households

How to foster this action:
- education on the financial and environmental benefits of energy-efficient products and training on installation, use and maintenance
- incentives and rewards to tradespeople to recommend and install energy-efficient products

Roles for the housing industry (architects, builders and tradespeople)
- designers and constructors of energy-efficient homes

How to foster this action:
- minimum standards for building envelopes (Given highly climate-related demand in SA, minimum standard should be 5-star national home energy rating system.)
- minimum standards for appliances installed at time of construction; priority be given to water heating (solar or 5-star gas as minimum), heating and cooling, water fittings (AAA as minimum) and lighting
- minimum energy-efficient standards for subdivisions

Roles for appliance manufacturers/importers
- provide energy-efficient appliances
- provide appliances that can easily be switched off (not just left on standby)

How to foster this action:
- minimum performance standards to be based on best practice
- specific performance standards for standby power
- research, development and commercialisation of next generation heating and cooling systems

Roles for state government

- encourage the roles of the stakeholders identified above
- provide for ongoing demand-side planning; this could occur through a recasting of the role and membership of the Electricity Supply Industry Planning Council or through the establishment of a sister body
- develop a demand-side management code of practice for electricity distributors, modelled on the NSW code
- advocate for reforms to the National Electricity Market that incorporate environmental externalities (such as the impacts of climate change and air pollution) into both the assessment of interconnectors and the price at which electricity is traded

Resourcing demand-side management

For purely economic reasons, demand-side management should be undertaken when it is a cheaper alternative to upgrading the electricity supply system. Such upgrades can occur at the distribution system, transmission system or with electricity generators. For example, if a component of the electrical distribution system, such as a substation, is no longer capable of meeting local electricity demands, then the distribution company has the option of either reducing the demand to meet the available capacity or augmenting the capacity.

The skills and participants required in the design and implementation of demand-side programs differ from those required to upgrade a distribution system. Hence, distribution companies are not necessarily ideally suited to considering demand-side responses.

To encourage other participants in demand-side initiatives, the NSW Ministry of Energy and Utilities has produced a demand-side management code of practice for electricity distributors.

To investigate how this code of practice could work, the NSW Sustainable Energy Development Authority (SEDA) undertook an analysis into demand-side alternatives to a proposed transformer upgrade in Cessnock, NSW. Avoiding the $8–10 million upgrade would save around $1 million per year in interest payments. And to do this would require implementing 2 megavolt-amp (MVA) (around 2 MW) of reduced demand. Hence demand-management options costing less than $500,000/MVA would be viable. The

SEDA study found that programs to encourage standby generation, interruptible loads, gas chillers, cogeneration, lighting retrofits, efficient refrigerators and gas turbines would all cost less than this.

As the Cessnock example shows, deferring network upgrades offers an opportunity to fund demand-side management programs. A similar approach can be taken to shortages in generation capacity.

The analysis of resourcing demand-side management described above is based on financially viable options. Such an assessment ignores the fact that environmental impacts, such as air pollution and greenhouse gas emissions from fossil fuel power plants, are not considered in the operations of the National Electricity Market. To gauge the scale of such 'externalities' one European study has found that the impacts of air pollution from coal-fired power plants are comparable to that which consumers pay for electricity. Including greenhouse gas impacts would make this figure higher.

Incorporating such externalities would make energy-efficiency options quite attractive and may well be cheaper than burning fossil fuels.

Conclusion

The current use and growth in use of fossil fuel-powered electricity in SA is both ecologically and economically unsustainable. The most cost-effective means of moving away from fossil fuel power is through demand-side management. Peak demand management can avoid short-term requirements for system augmentation and energy efficiency can offer long-term benefits.

One of the pioneers in demand-side management has been the US Rocky Mountains Institute (RMI). It is fitting to conclude a discussion on this topic with a quote from this organisation. The institute's web site (www.rmi.org) is an excellent place to discover more on this issue.

The inefficient use of energy causes many economic and security problems, and most environmental ones. Simply using energy in a way that saves money would avoid most of these problems. RMI therefore works to speed the free-market adoption of a 'soft energy path' – a profitable blending of efficient energy use with safe, sustainable sources to provide the same or better services while saving money, abating pollution and climate change, reducing the threat of nuclear proliferation, and increasing global security.

References

ABS (Australian Bureau of Statistics) 1999, *Environmental Issues – People's Views and Practices*, ABS, Canberra.

AGO (Australian Greenhouse Office) 2001, *Global Warming, Cool it!: A home guide to reducing energy costs and greenhouse gases*, AGO, Canberra, available at (http://www.greenhouse.gov.au/pubs/gwci/index.html)

Energy SA 1999, *Residential Energy Related Greenhouse Gas Emission*, Adelaide, available at http://www.sustainable.energy.sa.gov.au/pages/advisory/residential/energy_use/overview/pdf/greenhouse.pdf)

ESIPC (Electricity Supply Industry Planning Council) 2000, *Annual Planning Review*, ESIPC, Adelaide.

_____2001, *Annual Planning Review*, ESIPC, Adelaide, available at http://www.esipc. sa.gov.au/downloads/2001_APR_final_website.pdf

IPCC Working Group 1 2001, *Assessment Report: Summary for policy makers*, Shanghai draft 2001.

RMI (Rocky Mountains Institute) 2002, *RMI's Approach to Energy*, RMI, Colorado, available at http://www.rmi.org/sitepages/pid116.php

SEDA (Sustainable Energy Development Authority) 199?, *Home Cooling – Choosing a Cooling System*, NSW Sustainable Energy Development Authority, Sydney.

Disclaimer

This chapter has been prepared under the auspices of the Cool Communities Program. Cool Communities is an Australian Greenhouse Office (AGO) project delivered in collaboration with the Conservation Council of South Australia. The views expressed in this submission are not necessarily those of the AGO or any Cool Communities participating partners.

CHAPTER 10

Towards a Culture of Energy Efficiency

ANDREW NANCE

Introduction

Many people believe that technology will save us from our short-term dependence on fossil fuels and that these technologies will be widely applied when there's 'a buck in it' for the firms involved. But new technologies will only succeed when people choose to purchase or use them. Understanding how consumers relate to energy and having a sound knowledge of the barriers preventing people making good energy decisions are critical to ensuring that the objective of energy efficiency is widely practised in our society.

A sustainable energy future for South Australia will require energy efficiency to be part of our culture. Extracting the most from our resources and wasting nothing, must become the 'norm'. When a community culture of resource efficiency (energy, water, materials, land-use efficiency and so on) exists, voluntary programs can be extremely effective.

At this stage governments shouldn't be relying on markets to deliver energy efficiency. First of all the community needs to be educated to take responsibility for building a culture of energy efficiency. The most powerful interests in the market are primarily motivated to sell more and more energy, and it is only when people are aware of the energy consequences of their decisions and are in a position to affect the market, that energy markets are more likely to deliver the energy efficiency and consumer protection that is needed.

Encouraging the growth of this culture diverts discussion on energy away from economics and engineering into the realm of the social sciences. Behavioural change, community-based social marketing and related issues become integral to the electricity debate – in this instance, to the South Australian electricity debate.

This chapter is intended to be a reminder to policy-makers that, in the end, sustainable energy is not so much about technologies and the economics of markets as it is about people, the communities in which they live and the decisions they make.

Energy in society

Residential customers consume around one-third of the electricity sold in South Australia. And while appliances are becoming more energy-efficient, we are filling our homes and offices with more and more of them and building dwellings with scant regard for the ongoing costs (to the hip-pocket and the environment!) of living in them. On top of this, through the energy 'embodied' in the goods and services we consume (in the raw materials, processing, manufacturing and distribution), the residential consumer is indirectly responsible for most of the country's energy consumption.

We continue to consume energy at a growing rate and reducing this per-capita consumption is a prime objective of the demand-side management (DSM) initiatives identified earlier in this publication. We know that many opportunities exist for improved energy efficiency in the home, but how do we build a new culture, harness these opportunities and ensure widespread adoption of the technologies and practices presented?

Community-based social marketing (CBSM) is held up as an alternative to poorly targetted 'blanket' information campaigns. Using social science research as their basis, CBSM proponents believe widespread behavioural change is most effectively realised when delivered at the community level, and when initiatives have the dual focus of removing barriers to 'socially desirable' activities and enhancing the benefits and perceptions of these activities.

We have seen many successful social marketing initiatives in Australia that have sought behavioural change targeting a range of social activities; for example those which have urged a reduction in littering, smoking, drink driving and speeding. Successful public-awareness campaigns highlighting the dangers of unsafe sex, HIV/AIDS have also been run. Australia is recognised as a world leader in such campaigns and this provides an extremely sound base for marketing the sorts of changes in community attitudes and behaviour we're talking about.

Social research highlights the complexity of consumer behaviours and attitudes. Not everyone will be motivated to save energy solely for cost reasons and people will also be unwilling or unable to invest in energy efficiency for a number of reasons. The community needs strong leadership and concise, concrete information on reducing energy consumption delivered through effective public awareness and support programs. In this respect the evidence indicates that person-to-person contact and hands-on experience may be the most effective means of delivery.

Energy action

Recognising the impact that DSM has on the objectives of meeting greenhouse reduction targets, the Australian Greenhouse Office (AGO) has been exploring the small but growing global body of research and experience relating to energy use by societies.

Energy efficiency sits alongside transport as a prime target in the National Greenhouse Strategy and the AGO has been investigating the effective and ineffective elements of many of the social marketing campaigns noted above and how they might be applied to marketing 'greenhouse-friendly' decision-making to the wider community.

One important and practical contribution to understanding household energy behaviour is the 2000 title, *Motivating Home Energy Action: A handbook of what works*, written by Michelle Shipworth for the AGO. It provides a useful review of worldwide research into household energy behaviour and reminds us that home energy action is concerned as much with attitudes as with technology. It uses social science insights into people's behaviour to recommend home energy action programs which, it is hoped, will prove to be effective.

Shipworth identifies the following categories as the basis for home energy action programs:

- attitudes sometimes motivate
- information sometimes motivates
- money sometimes motivates
- people need people

Attitudes

Many people display a strong and positive 'environmental attitude', yet this is often contradicted by their behaviour. While most of us know better we continue to waste energy, sometimes knowingly, sometimes not.

Motivation to change can be lessened by fear of inconvenience arising from lifestyle changes and a lack of time to wade through energy-saving information and strategies. In short it can all appear to be just too hard.

Shipworth (2000) strongly advocates the effectiveness of 'foot in the door' strategies, where small experiences, good or bad, are amplified. This approach is supported by case studies highlighting the value of hands-on trials and demonstrations.

One of the major barriers to change identified by the AGO is lack of access to energy-saving alternatives. Changing attitudes will only have minimal effect if choices are limited, difficult to access or just not available at all. Fostering the development of suppliers of energy-efficient products and services therefore forms part of an overall strategy. This is a reminder that the 'energy consequences' of our lifestyles are often outside our direct control.

Several studies also demonstrate that differences in consumption patterns are often linked more to cultural differences than to differences in attitudes to energy and the environment, a fact illustrated by Shipworth through the media coverage of the 1998 Victorian natural gas crisis where it became clear that there is a strong cultural relationship between Australians and hot showers. Recognising that water heating is the single largest end-use of energy in the home, it is clear that reducing hot water energy use is imperative. Thus any initiatives in this area must account for the Australian pattern of behaviour. In this context it is possible that a barrier to the uptake of solar water heaters is the perception that hot water will run short in winter. If this is a widely held perception, then it is worthwhile utilising a financial incentive to promote the uptake of solar hot water, as well as tailoring marketing to allay these fears.

Information

Although an essential component strategy of any program, information alone will inspire little if any home energy action. Generic information programs are not effective, whereas comprehensive programs with multiple strategies are.

As evidenced over the summer of 2001–02 at a series of well-attended energy-use forums in Adelaide, there appears to be a hunger in the community for information about energy efficiency. These served to highlight the importance of effective delivery of information, the need to recognise very different levels of information held by people and the value of receiving information from credible sources. Plumbers, electricians, appliance retailers, community groups and social networks have proved to be very effective elements of home energy action programs as they can provide this credibility. An effective strategy would involve close collaboration with groups such as these and would assume the provision of appropriate training to enable them to provide advice.

Simple, low-cost, low-effort, 'hands-on' experiences can reinforce energy-efficiency messages. Since people need to be able to interact with the technology and get a feel for it, these events need to be more than just slide shows. South Australia's energy information centres have an array of brochures and friendly staff but no technology to play with! One option might be the establishment of a combined government–industry centre that enabled interaction with renewable energy and energy-efficiency equipment, viewing of live demonstrations and practical advice.

Other local activities, such as energy workshops at hardware stores on weekends, might suit some people, while others may prefer more direct 'in-home' advice and help. Community-based programs which recognise these diverse preferences are essential.

The AGO's research clearly demonstrates that community members want meaningful information to enable them to act. The challenge is to meet this need in an innovative and flexible way.

Money

All people are different and all have varying abilities to change their decisions and become more energy-efficient. Technical discussions often present more than the usual language barriers but access to capital is often one of the biggest barriers of all.

Classical economic theory often does a disservice to people's relationships with money. The underlying assumption is that people will act in a rational manner and place a reasonable value on savings over time from an upfront investment. When investment in energy-efficient solutions does not occur, economists often argue that the benefits to the community are overstated – 'if it was that good it would be happening already'.

Many 'big-ticket' efficiency gains require an initial outlay of money, with the cost recovered through saved energy bills over a period of, usually, two or more years. Solar water heaters are a good example of this. Simple financial incentive schemes (such as subsidies and rebates) may target these barriers but can result in poor participation for a number of reasons:

- Householders are rarely aware of which appliances or features of their homes are the major contributors to their energy costs. Making the most cost-effective decisions is difficult for many.

- Average home energy expenditure is relatively small (usually well below 5% of income) and roughly equates to average expenditure on alcohol. It is not an economic priority for many households. For many others however, energy costs make up a much larger percentage of a limited household income but these are the same households which are most often unable to raise any capital at all. Even subsidised costs are unattainable.

- Non-financial aspects, such as how well the incentive is promoted and the relative ease with which it can be accessed, contribute to success.

- Payback periods on (subsidised) capital investments are still often considered unacceptable. For example, most solar water heaters will have recouped their initial cost in energy savings years before their warranty expires yet they represent only a few per cent of the water heating market!

There is certainly scope for more innovative ways of financing energy actions, particularly those based on using the value of energy savings to purchase or lease efficient appliances. This practice is becoming increasingly available to industry and businesses but is a rare option for households.

Research has also been conducted which supports claims that middle- and high-income households are more likely to be receptive to once-off purchasing, while behavioural-change initiatives are more likely to achieve success with low-income households, the elderly and others with little or no access to capital. A rebate program with one set of inflexible rules is therefore likely to target only a narrow group of people.

Increasing energy prices is regarded by many as a key strategy for changing attitudes to energy. It is argued that per-unit energy prices should reflect the full cost of supply, including any environmental and public health impact. Efficiency gains are then used to restrain increases in overall energy cost. (Per-unit prices increase but the number of units required falls, and ideally a balance is achieved.) There is little or no evidence, however, that in isolation, a 20% increase in electricity prices would result in, say, 20% less consumption. This 'inelastic' behaviour of energy supply is well known, and to achieve desired efficiency gains, price signals to influence behaviour must be accompanied by sufficient support programs.

It is truly one of the most unfortunate results of the 'dis-integration' of the electricity supply industry that we now rely on the market to allocate capital, with the result that there is significant investment in more supply but very little investment in end-use efficiency. And it is easy to understand why, since the supply-side investment is ultimately recouped from the consumer by the supply industry, but demand-side activities result in savings flowing to the consumers!

Cost-effectiveness

The nature of energy use and the many variables influencing it make the effectiveness of programs difficult to measure. Despite this difficulty it will be increasingly necessary to develop appropriate measures of the cost-effectiveness of energy-efficiency programs in order to justify the funding allocated to them. A report presented to the World Solar Congress in 2001 by Energy SA suggests that little attention has been paid to the development of such measures. Measurement difficulties therefore present significant barriers to home energy action programs.

Significant barriers to consumer understanding of the impact of their energy-use behaviour also exist. We are presently billed quarterly for actions occurring months earlier. New electricity meters may well provide instantaneous information about electricity-usage cost, but it appears that this will not prove to be the solution, since research indicates that some householders presented with real-time cost information tend to use more energy. Their quarterly bill still provided a shock but the incremental costs made electricity seem quite cheap! (Shipworth 2000).

People

A significant body of research highlights the value of person-to-person contact in encouraging positive actions (Shipworth 2000). This includes concepts such as 'adaptive muddling' (householders are encouraged to experiment), competition between groups (to reach energy-saving targets) and the importance of public displays of commitment (such as solar water heaters, publishing the names of committed householders in local papers, stickers on letterboxes or signs in householders' windows).

This is, of course, consistent with the desire to establish a culture of energy efficiency – where the people in the community share a commitment to energy efficiency. This culture 'spreads the word' through credible sources, has local champions and active social networks advocating and practising energy efficiency.

Conclusion

Energy is vital to the wellbeing of society, yet we have an energy system which responds inadequately to community and environmental concerns. The electricity market in particular must be geared to the achievement of the objective of sustainability. Domestic consumers, alongside small businesses, commercial and industrial operations must develop a culture of energy efficiency and take control of their energy use. This culture should be underpinned by an ethos of waste minimalisation as well as the provision of equitable access to energy.

It is incumbent upon government and the public sector to provide leadership and build on initiatives like those emerging from the AGO. In the end, the engagement of local communities is essential in building a culture of energy efficiency. Well-designed home-energy action programs are likely to be a key ingredient in achieving this objective.

There is considerable evidence that comprehensive programs with multiple strategies work best. Case studies illustrate the need to engage the many stakeholders – manufacturers, salespeople, communities, consumers etc. They also demonstrate the need for the adoption of different strategies for the wide diversity of consumers, not merely the diversity of their incomes. These programs are also seen as those most likely to result in 'market transformation' from the current 'niche' market for sustainable energy and energy-efficiency products and services to the situation where energy efficiency and sustainability become the 'norm'.

Useful websites

Australian Greenhouse Office Community Awareness Research
(National Greenhouse Strategy) publications available at
http://www.greenhouse.gov.au/ pubs/community.html

Shipworth, Michelle 2000, *Motivating Home Energy Action: A handbook of what works*, Australian Greenhouse Office, Canberra.

Community-based social marketing website available at www.cbsm.org

Tools of change website available at www.toolsofchange.com

CHAPTER 11

Energy and Equity

Towards a socially responsible energy policy*

JOHN LAWRENCE

Introduction

Energy policy in South Australia should be governed by a set of principles which extend beyond the narrow confines of short-term economic rationalist objectives to include those of equity and social justice. In a community experiencing a growing disparity between rich and poor and rising numbers of people in relative poverty, specific energy policy measures are required to protect the interests of the most vulnerable and to improve the living standards of low-income households.

The introduction of 'full retail contestability' (FRC) for residential consumers in the local electricity market is likely to have consequences which measures such as these should address. Significant electricity tariff increases of 20% and more are widely expected to accompany full contestability, at least in the initial years of implementation. From a longitudinal perspective, these tariff rises come on top of higher base tariffs and adverse long-term consumer price index (CPI) trends in this state. In October 2001 the *Advertiser* reported that the Electricity Supply Association of Australia claimed that, over the last decade, South Australian household electricity prices have been some 12% above national average prices. Moreover, recent Australian Bureau of Statistics (ABS) CPI data also demonstrate that local Adelaide electricity bills have increased at the second

---

* This chapter is based on research undertaken by the author as part of the Low Income Energy Consumers Project of the SA Council of Social Service, funded by the Essential Services Commission of South Australia.

highest rate among Australian capital cities, behind only Hobart (and Darwin for gas). The weighted increase was 41.7 CPI points compared with a national average increase of 29.9 points. Furthermore, electricity was among the highest item increases in the CPI over this period, alongside transport and health costs.

Because they command a larger proportion of their total household expenditure, such changes tend to have the greatest impact on the household budgets and lives of the poorest in this state. Furthermore, those living in this income bracket are usually least able to gain additional funds to compensate for these increases. Financial pressures like these are also likely to occur in a complex social and psychological context of poverty, affecting and being shaped by factors such as low education levels, low morale and under-resourced support structures. A disability pensioner with dependants for example, may have limited literacy and numeracy capabilities, be severely depressed about his or her circumstances, and be socially isolated by poverty. These experiences are both accentuated by major energy price increases and reduce the individual and household ability to manage such price increases effectively.

To address this fundamental and growing problem of energy-linked social injustice, this chapter advocates a South Australian energy policy based on strong equity principles. It draws from recent local research undertaken by the author, in the Low Income Electricity Consumers (LIEC) project, to identify the key electricity issues affecting low-income households, and makes some recommendations on how these issues can be resolved. While the focus here is on electricity policy, a parallel case can readily be made for gas supply. An equitable energy policy for this state must integrate these analyses if it is to offer a sufficiently comprehensive approach to these issues.

Key principles for an equitable state energy policy

The Oxford Dictionary defines 'equity' as 'that which is fair and right' and the 'recourse to general principles of justice to correct or supplement ordinary law'.

In the case of energy policy, this equity principle has both protective and redistributive elements. The application of this principle for example, should ensure that the most vulnerable in our community are protected from excessive corporate profiteering, bullying tactics in extracting debt repayment and the adverse consequences of supply disconnection.

The redistributive element of an equitable energy policy has a complementary function. Given the growing importance of electricity to the maintenance of a basic standard of living in our community in particular, access to this energy source should be regarded a fundamental right, not a privilege reserved for those who can afford it most readily. In applying this principle, all households should be guaranteed access; for example, to appropriate warmth in winter and cooling in summer, that is, meeting fundamental human physical needs alongside those of adequate shelter, food and clothing. In the case of low-income households, the accompanying responsibility to make payments for this supply should in turn reflect their capacity to pay for their energy needs, with redistributive measures such as adequate concessions, emergency payments and subsidised energy conservation devices available to underpin this principle. Withdrawal of supply (that is, disconnection) should only be used as a measure of last resort for the small numbers of consumers refusing to pay rather than a punishment for those unable to pay in the short or longer term.

For the purposes of our discussion, 'electricity equity' can be considered as including these protective and redistributive elements.

The experience of low-income households

According to research published by the South Australian Council of Social Services (SACOSS) in 2001, 11.8% (approximately 70,000) of South Australian households live in poverty after housing costs are taken into account (Carson & Martin 1991). Those most at risk include single people aged between 21 and 24, couples with one, two or three dependent children, sole parents with two or more children and aged people in private rental dwellings. Many other households in or near the lowest 20% of income earners have been increasingly 'doing it tough' over recent years. All these low-income households are likely to experience significant inequity in relation to accessing electricity.

In a low-income electricity consumer (LIEC) household, an

electricity bill is usually part of a complex set of financial challenges generated by insufficient income for a household to meet expenditure demands. The LIEC project research suggests however, that electricity (and gas) bills have increasingly become 'the final straw' factor, the trigger for a financial crisis in that household.

LIEC households value electricity as a key part of 'surviving' and clinging to some basic standard of living (that is, heating, cooling, hot water, lighting, cooking and TV). They fear disconnection as a dramatic further blow to this basic and familiar standard. They also recognise the importance of electricity in sustaining health and wellbeing – creating a sufficient level of personal comfort for each resident, for example, to manage the symptoms of asthma, epilepsy, depression and acute family stress. As one focus group participant in the LIEC project commented:

I'd go crazy if I didn't have cooling, I really would . . . On my medication I can't seem to keep cool, I can't sleep in the hot weather . . . Without the cooler I'd argue all the time with my partner . . . and the kids would cop it . . . its not fair on them.

In the unequal society we live in, the poor are often criticised for being improvident with their limited resources, while the community at large is regularly encouraged to consume more for the 'sake of the economy'. It is important to recognise here that the expectations of a 'basic standard of living' are changing and along with them, expectations of basic energy needs.

Low-income households are unable to reduce energy consumption easily without a major decline in their basic living standards. Houses and the appliances used in them are usually older and less energy-efficient and their inhabitants very aware of cost and consumption. Furthermore, many special energy demands are health-imposed (for example, heating and cooling of the elderly, the sick and babies, equipment for chronic illnesses). Members of LIEC households are often forced, for financial reasons, to stay at home during the day, using heating, cooling and other electrical equipment during peak tariff hours. The more affluent working population tends to enjoy the benefit of employers covering such costs.

Consumers on low incomes are unlikely to accumulate financial reserves and unexpected, imposed expenditure items regularly create household financial crises. In such circumstances, bills are routinely juggled, with repayments renegotiated and postponed. A retailer debt-recovery strategy geared to more affluent customers often fails to recognise and respond appropriately to this reality. Moreover, disconnection and reconnection fees simply deepen the debt problems faced by these low-income households.

Many LIEC households also appear to be intimidated by the increasingly 'tough attitude' of the energy retailers (that is, electricity and gas) to bill repayments. There is considerable local anecdotal evidence of customers facing hard, rigid and dismissive responses from some staff on the customer service desk to their requests for repayment extensions. For many, already with low morale, lacking confidence and with limited negotiating skills, this can be a gruelling and frustrating experience. More and more welfare agency staff are being called upon to intervene – and usually with better success rates.

Support services are increasingly feeling the consequences of this growing difficulty paying utilities' bills. Financial counsellors and emergency relief staff for example, are reporting growing numbers and new groups (for example, young men) 'burying their pride' and asking for help to manage electricity bills (or food, when energy bill payment has depleted the household budget). For these services, and especially emergency relief, client electricity bills are generating a new challenge on top of their long-term struggle to stretch very limited agency budgets. Simultaneously, many of these agencies are battling with large rises in their own electricity bills as a result of retail contestability. Without additional funding, their only alternative is to reduce services and more tightly ration welfare provision.

Much community education and information dealing with debt management and energy conservation is inappropriate for a wide range of low-income households since it inaccurately assumes a level of education, a physical and mental capacity, sufficient affluence, and sustained, confidently proactive attitudes. Further, social service agencies promoting information in these sorts of areas are often 'preaching to the converted'. Thus the greatest benefits are realised by the relatively better-off sections of the community rather than those most in need of such services.

With the rapid growth in the purchase and use of reverse-cycle air conditioners over the last five years, South Australia has experienced a substantial growth in summer electricity demand. This in turn requires electricity retailers (principally AGL over recent years) to purchase extremely expensive electricity from peaking plants and other National Grid sources in order to maintain supply obligations. As these costs are subsequently transferred to customers as an averaged price per unit over the billing cycle, high-end customers (that is, those using large cooling systems and extensively on hot days), usually the more affluent, are cross-subsidised by lower-use consumers with less of this equipment and less capacity to afford it.

Finally, key energy-conservation measures, such as adequate insulation, draught prevention and shading, and solar hot water systems are least likely to be installed in cheaper homes and rental properties. Nor are low-income consumers often able to afford many of the measures recommended in energy-conservation campaigns, further reducing their capacity to reduce energy bills.

Diversity of household electricity experiences

Additional factors have been identified affecting specific groups of LIEC households from this energy equity perspective. As part of a process to tailor state energy policy to meet the diverse needs of low-income households each should be considered.

Geography and seasonality

The particular demands on energy consumption (both cooling and heating) and therefore bill difficulties experienced by LIEC households living in the more extreme climatic zones of this state deserve more equitable recognition in public energy policy. The SA Housing Trust has recognised this factor in its prioritising of certain regions for retrofitted insulation of housing stock.

Age

Many young LIEC households are attempting to survive on very low incomes. Some appear to extend their financial difficulties through inexperience, poor judgement and through the lack of household management and negotiating skills. 'Middle-aged' LIEC households often support families and thus may face greater difficulties in reining in household electricity consumption (for example, with more complex energy demands, child health problems etc.). On the other hand, this group may possess better management and negotiation skills, acquired through experience. The impact of disconnection on these invariably larger households will obviously affect more people and may be greater as a result. Older LIEC households appear to be motivated by a sense of responsibility to pay their utility bills even if this results in reduced expenditure on other core items such as food.

Mental illness

In the LIEC project, a range of community agencies indicated that mental illness is a recognised cause of client problems, including those of budgeting, managing utilities' bills and negotiating effectively on bill payment. A person with a severe mental illness is often readily and extremely distressed, suffers memory loss and has an inability to organise the responsibilities of their daily lives. In this state, they are reliant on finding a capable and committed advocate to negotiate on their behalf with the utility companies.

Aboriginality

As with many other social problems, Aboriginal people are disproportionately represented amongst those experiencing LIEC difficulties. These difficulties include an unfamiliarity with the requirements of urban living, the cultural obligation to provide for extended family visitors for a length of time and the notably higher rates of physical and mental health problems, all of which generate higher demands for energy consumption and lowered capacity to manage payment for it.

Policy directions

Addressing the common and specific problems of LIEC households requires a diverse and integrated range of strategies. These should include consideration of the following.

Price capping

In the short term this measure is essential to protect LIECs from the expected initial surges in electricity tariffs associated with the introduction of the fully contestable retail market.

Multi-tiered tariff structure

To provide incentives for lowering household consumption, tariff levels could be differentiated by, for example, a taxation-style set of price brackets or the use of excess charges for consumption over a certain limit.

Concession arrangements

A review of current concession policy is urgently needed to ensure adequate levels of support for those most in need. This review should include the Emergency Electricity Payments Scheme and consideration of benchmarking against interstate best practices.

Consumer retail code

The code which governs retailers' practice should in particular, ensure a consumer's 'right to supply' (that is, that all households are entitled to the provision of electricity), effective debt-management strategies, and responsible advertising and sales practices. An unmandated uptake of innovative programs developed by some retailers would also be welcomed. Aurora Energy (Tasmania) for example, has shown a real commitment to helping LIECs through early identification of customer debt problems (and offering them appropriate repayment plans), minimising disconnections and building rapport, using home visits, with debt-problem customers.

Customer sale contracts

A standard contract should be available within the retail code, one which offers a basic benchmark for other contracts and a well-promoted 'fall-back position' for those inexperienced and uncertain in the new contestable market. All contracts should be independently regulated for the use of clear, carefully worded and straightforward language. Some provisions proposed in the standard code should remain mandatory for all contracts in order to protect vulnerable customers from exploitative sales staff.

Service standards and a customer charter

A clear statement of customer service standards and the penalties attached to lapses is a useful, public display of a retailer's service commitment, one which provides a clarification of the service a customer can anticipate, and perhaps most importantly, a means by which service performance can be publicly monitored and potentially improved. Similarly, a customer charter offers customers an open statement of the rights and obligations of both parties in any contract. Both of these documents (service standards and the customer charter) need to be easy to read and made readily available to customers. Well-designed and graphic brochures provided to all prospective customers on request and to all new customers should be a basic requirement within the retail code. This is particularly important to some low-income customers who may face literacy and/or English language comprehension difficulties. Such documents should be seen as part of a community obligation from retailers – to help build fundamental consumer understanding of this new, competitive market, to enable transparent comparisons to be made between competing retailers and to reduce the incidence of poor service and other consumer difficulties. For low-income consumers with higher rates of problem-related contact with their retailer, the benefits of this strategy should be self-evident.

Community education for 'full retail contestability' (FRC)

Drawing from the UK and Victorian experience of retail electricity privatisation, publicity and public education are urgently required to allay fears about cost increases and to ensure that the proposed benefits of retail choice are delivered to all residential households. Graphic presentations and TV campaigns will be needed for this purpose.

Consumer debt-management education and information strategies

A review of electricity and generic debt management strategies would provide a useful adjunct to the above initiative, resulting in improved delivery of these strategies alongside those for FRC.

Household energy audits

Free household energy audits need to be made available to LIECs, along with advice on and provision of low-cost measures to reduce energy waste. Internationally, energy and water utilities are beginning to recognise this as a cost-effective approach to reducing peak summer demand and supply problems, to lowering the costs of debt recovery and to building positive community recognition. A project managed by the Newcastle City Council in the Hunter region is demonstrating the opportunities for creating similar outcomes here in South Australia. Advice on the efficient use of electricity needs to be delivered in formats appropriate to and effective with the target audiences. Generic advertising campaigns are not sufficient and recent UK research suggests that LIECs will best respond to personal contact from community-based 'energy advisors'.

Other conservation measures

Better consumer control of household electricity usage can play an important part in managing the impact of price increases on low-income households. Measures to support this approach should include both grants and subsidies for the installation of low-cost energy conservation measures in low-income private and public housing. In this latter case, 'AAA' showerheads, flow restrictors, draught and shading devices and insulation can dramatically lower heating and cooling costs. This recommendation has become increasingly important in light of the evidence suggesting that recent bill rises reported by low-income households appear primarily the result of increased consumption rather than tariff price rises. Additional benefits of such measures include reducing summer peak demand levels as well as reducing the production of greenhouse gases in the state and national electricity grid.

Centrepay

From October 2001, Centrelink has offered automatic deductions from government benefit payments to cover electricity bills. This arrangement appears to be the one significant, recent innovation to offer major benefits to LIECs and has received strong support from this population group in SA over recent months. Clients with addictive behaviours (gambling, drugs, alcohol etc.) are reported to be most advantaged by this scheme. While the impact of this initiative on remaining essential expenditure items (for example, food, clothing, health and transport) and reduced flexibility of household financial management will require further enquiry, this service appears to deserve promotion as an option for all low-income households.

Electricity Industry Ombudsman

Adequate promotion of this service to all LIECs is also required as a means of improving dispute resolution without further penalties or disconnection.

Corporate customer service officer training

Improved complaints and dispute-resolution procedures, including staff training, which take the realities of LIECs into account and which are reflected in service standards would be an encouraging improvement.

Smart-card metering

This means of collecting payments using prepayment on a credit-type card loaded into the household meter is currently being trialled in SA. It may offer significant benefits to some consumers, including closer monitoring of expenditure and better consumption management. However, it is also creating a number of concerns. These include the cost of purchase and installation of the card-reading equipment, the potential for requiring some households to install them as a condition of supply, and limiting competition by blocking exit and entry and access by third parties to confidential information. Most disturbing of all perhaps is the potential for household self-disconnections due to poverty and which go unrecorded by the utility or government.

Conclusion

Low-income electricity households in South Australia will continue to be treated inappropriately under the energy policies of this state unless a comprehensive approach is developed which includes strong and consistent equity principles. This chapter has outlined a broad framework for developing such an approach.

References

Carson, E & Martin, S 1991, *Social Disadvantage in South Australia*, SA
    Council of Social Service, Adelaide.

CHAPTER 12

In the Public Interest

Strategies for civic engagement in the electricity industry

KATHRYN DAVIDSON AND JOHN SPOEHR

Introduction

The introduction of full retail contestability (FRC) in 2003 exposes small consumers to a market-based electricity industry with few opportunities for informed consumer feedback on the operation of the system as a whole. There is a great need for consumers to be able to participate in shaping the operation of the market, particularly because of the social and environmental implications inherent in electricity systems.

Because of its complexity, it is vital that consumers have the ability to make informed choices and decisions about the market. To do this consumers need to be well-equipped with high-quality analysis of market trends, issues and social and environmental impacts. This chapter will argue the requirement for developing more effective structures to address consumer and environmental concerns in the South Australian electricity market. It will review a number of local and overseas models designed to achieve this objective before outlining some options for improving consumer participation in the South Australia electricity market.

Electricity is an essential service

Effective representation of consumer and environmental interests in shaping the operation and outcomes of the electricity industry is linked to the central role that electricity plays in Australian society. Electricity is essential for the maintenance of our social, physical and economic wellbeing. Many of the technologies used in our daily lives are powered by electricity. The functioning of hospitals, schools, businesses, homes, transportation and communication systems depends upon the availability of electricity. Electricity cannot be easily substituted by other forms of energy, although gas remains a limited alternative.

The movement towards a market-based electricity system fundamentally changes the mechanisms available for public accountability in the electricity industry. This is particularly so in South Australia where the industry has been privatised. Now that the assets are in private hands, the South Australian community no longer has direct influence over the operation of the industry. A complex web of regulatory structures influences the operation of the market. Currently there is very limited consumer involvement in these structures.

With South Australian residential and small business entering the contestable market on 1 January 2003, the immediate focus of public concern is upon price outcomes and reliability of supply during the summer months. Most attention in dealing with these concerns has been upon increasing supply rather than reducing demand. Issues such as the impact of rising prices on low-income consumers and environmental imperatives have been sidelined. In the absence of significant reform to the electricity market it is likely that the big losers will be residential consumers, particularly those on low incomes, and the environment. Lack of attention in the current market-based system to issues of equity and environmental sustainability necessitate the introduction of mechanisms and structures to ensure that the electricity industry is more publicly accountable and responsive. We will explore some of the options in the following sections.

Residential consumers and the South Australian electricity market

Residential consumers generally have less bargaining power in relation to price outcomes and other matters than do business and government consumers. Influence in a market-based system is related to consumption levels, with large consumers of electricity generally being able to bargain for better price outcomes. When they don't achieve the price objectives they seek, some large consumers are in a position to establish their own generation capacity. Clearly this is not an option at the moment for most residential consumers. Large electricity consumers tend to be well represented in negotiations with the industry – through business associations, energy-user alliances and hired lobbyists. It is difficult for residential consumers to influence the market because of the complexity of the issues involved, the time and financial commitment required and the lack of advocacy support available.

Appropriate mechanisms need to be developed within the electricity market to overcome barriers to small consumer participation. The development of an end-user's advocacy network/organisation would be a worthwhile start. The objectives of such a body might include:

- representing end-users in the decision-making processes within the industry
- informing and educating end-users about the market
- conducting ongoing research and policy studies on issues specifically relevant to the end-user
- identifying and addressing systemic issues across the electricity market
- ensuring that consumer protection mechanisms work effectively.

Other mechanisms which might also be considered to invite consumer involvement include:

- establishing a university-based research centre on energy and consumer issues
- ensuring that small consumers are represented on all governing and/or decision-making bodies in the market. Sitting fees need to be provided to those involved, along with assistance in the analysis of industry trends and issues.

There are few avenues available in South Australia for detailed consideration of the social and environmental implications of the operation of the electricity market in the state. Soon after its election, the new state Labor Government created the role of the South Australian

Essential Services Commissioner (ESC). The ESC is an 'economic' regulator. The commissioner has a limited mandate to deal with social and environmental issues. This differs from the NSW energy regulator which has statutory obligations to consider social and environmental questions. The government has also established a Consumer Advisory Panel, chaired by Professor Richard Blandy. The panel provides representation for a range of groups, although its main focus seems to be on pricing issues, particularly as they impact upon larger consumers. The powers of these bodies could be augmented to provide a focus for discussions and recommendations relating to social and environmental issues.

Currently in South Australia there is a range of non-government organisations such as the South Australian Council of Social Service, the South Australian Council on the Ageing, the United Trades and Labor Council and the Conservation Council of South Australia, all of which are active in raising consumer and environmental issues related to the industry. None of these organisations is specifically resourced for this purpose, nor do they have the necessary expertise. Nonetheless, there are continual demands placed on these organisations to participate in the various working parties, steering committees and advisory groups. Although the burden of representation is eased for some representatives through the payment of sitting fees, consumer representatives go unsupported in attempting to come to grips with the complexities of the emerging market. There is a pressing need therefore for advocacy and research support to be provided to consumer and environmental interest groups to ensure that they are able to participate in an informed manner.

The need for mechanisms to facilitate effective participation by consumer and environmental groups in the decision-making structures of the industry should not be confused with existing state government-funded mechanisms providing for consumer complaints and dispute resolution. These functions are the responsibility of the Independent Electricity Ombudsman. What is being proposed here is an independent energy industry research and advocacy function designed to support the representation of small consumers and environmental interests.

Experience in other states

New South Wales

With full retail contestability (FRC) having been implemented in NSW and Victoria, South Australia is able to learn from past attempts to facilitate small consumer participation in electricity markets. A number of consumer initiatives in NSW and Victoria are worth investigating.

A research and advocacy capacity for small electricity consumers has existed in NSW for many years. In 1998 the Public Interest Advocacy Centre (PIAC) established the Utilities Consumer Advocacy Project (UCAP). The project is funded by the NSW State Government through the Minister of Energy and Utilities and has a broad mandate to represent the interests of residential consumers of gas, electricity and water services.

Significant resources have been allocated by the NSW Government to the establishment and operation of the Sustainable Energy Development Authority (SEDA). Established in 1996, SEDA's mission involves: 'Delivering greenhouse gas reductions, environmental, economic and social benefits to the NSW community by accelerating the transition to sustainable production and use of energy' (www.seda.nsw.gov.au). The establishment of SEDA has the potential to place NSW at the forefront of the development of sustainable energy production and use.

Victoria

There is a long history of electricity consumer advocacy in Victoria through the Energy Action Group (EAG) established in 1978–9. The EAG has received funding from a variety of sources, including philanthropic trusts, the Victorian Council of Social Service, the Council for Self Help Groups (a Victorian Government-funded public resource centre), and the Department of Energy and Minerals via a levy on the State Electricity Commission of Victoria (SECV) and the Gas & Fuel Corporation (GFC). Since 1997 total annual funding has fallen to only $1000 per annum. The Consumer Law Centre also plays some role in energy consumer advocacy.

In April 2002 the Victorian Minister for Energy and the Minister for Consumer Affairs announced the establishment of the

Consumer Utilities Advocacy Centre (CUAC). The centre will receive around $500,000 annually from the Victorian Government. Approximately $170,000 of this amount is expected to be distributed to other organisations and consultants to fund research and advocacy projects. The role of the centre is to undertake research and advocacy in the gas, water and electricity industries. The government has appointed a board for the centre and a reference group of consumer representatives will assist the board in determining the centre's strategic direction and priorities.

Overseas experience
United States of America
The US has a long history of consumer advocacy. This is reflected in legislation and funding made available for advocacy. Such is the importance of advocacy in the US that funding is made available for end-user advocacy in 46 of the 50 states (Pareto Associates 2000). Broadly, the different types of US electricity advocacy models are:

- state advocacy office
- intervenor
- standing bodies
- non-profit organisations, for example, National Consumer Law Centre and Consumer Federation of America
- non-advocacy, university-based centres and government agencies involved in education and research on topics related to the electricity industry.

State advocacy offices
The state advocacy offices (SAO) are located within and funded by state governments. They are an integral part of the industry, designated by state legislation to represent the interests of utility consumers before state and federal regulators and in the courts (Pareto Associates 2000).

In 2000 state-funded advocacy offices had been established in 39 states and the District of Columbia. Furthermore, intervenor compensation is also provided in 29 of these states. In addition, four states (California, Illinois, New York and Rhode Island) also have local government and/or privately funded advocacy offices. The latter have not been created by state law nor have statewide authority (Pareto Associates 2000).

Consumer advocate offices operate independently from the regulatory commissions in their states and are authorised by state law to act as ratepayer advocates. Broadly, the four types of SAO models are:

- staff situated in the attorney general's office, for example, the State of Minnesota
- a separate division within a regulatory agency, for example, California has a division called the Office of Ratepayer Advocates
- within the state regulator, staff (but not a separate division) specifically authorised to advocate on behalf of a subset of ratepayers
- a separate state office, created for the advocacy purpose or a new office within an existing state agency (not the Attorney General's office).

Intervenor model

The intervenor model makes funding available to enhance end-user advocacy. It includes the provision of funding to support participation in the energy industry.

For example, a regulatory agency may authorise and support a fund that distributes to consumers' or end-users' organisations for the purpose of technical and legal support for advocacy. This fund is administered and awards the funding through a board composed of consumer representatives.

Standing models

Standing models refer to the ongoing involvement of end-users' representations in the decision-making authority.

Non-profit consumer advocacy organisations

An example of a non-profit consumer advocacy organisation includes 'Public Citizen'. Public Citizen is a national, non-profit consumer advocacy organisation with national divisions in areas such as vehicle safety, Congress Watch, critical mass energy and environment program, global trade watch, health research, litigation and power resources. 'Buyers Up' division, covering power resources, assists consumers to pool their buying power and save money on home heating oil.

Public Citizen is funded through individual membership fees, bequests, publication sales and through support by philanthropic trusts. They do not accept funding from governments or the corporate sector (www.citizen.org).

United Kingdom

In the United Kingdom the recognition and role of consumer advocacy for energy and other utilities is legislated within the *Utilities Act 2000*, under which the statutory functions and duties of energywatch, the independent gas and electricity consumer council, is governed.

In the UK there are a number of organisations which represent the interest of consumers. Three of these organisations, the National Consumer Council, energywatch and the National Energy Action are described below.

National Consumer Council

The objectives of the National Consumer Council (NCC) are to:

- create smart, streetwise, skilled consumers by promoting access to high-quality education, information and advice
- develop markets and public services that work for everyone by finding the right balance between free markets, regulation and self-regulation
- provide solutions to the problems of exclusion by tackling the barriers that put goods and services out of reach
- ensure decision-makers everywhere are consumer-aware by strengthening consumer representation
- achieve the right balance between innovation and consumer protection by improving the understanding, communication and management of risk and uncertainty.

The NCC receives 81% of its income from a grant-in-aid from the Department of Trade and Industry.

energywatch

energywatch is an independent gas and electricity consumer council established by the *Utilities Act 2000*. energywatch is a national body which has regional and national offices in Scotland and Wales and is independent of OFGEM, the gas and electricity regulator.

energywatch aims to provide advice, information and advocacy services to consumers, and deals with complaints through a one-stop service. Furthermore, energywatch has a duty to represent the interests of disadvantaged consumers, including the disabled, the chronically ill, those on low incomes, the elderly and those residing in rural areas.

Funding is provided through the Department of Trade and Industry and is funded by the licence fees paid by suppliers, shippers, distributors, gas transporters and the electricity transmission licence holder to OFGEM.

National Energy Action

National Energy Action (NEA) aims to eradicate fuel poverty and campaigns for greater investment in energy efficiency to help those who are poor or vulnerable. NEA undertakes research and analysis, provides advice and guidance, develops and promotes energy-efficiency services and produces educational resources. It works in partnership with central and local government, with fuel utilities, housing providers and health services, and with consumer organisations.

NEA receives funding from the UK Government and it seeks sponsorship from energy companies and support from charitable trusts, as well as receiving fees from selling consultancy and training services.

Some implications of overseas experience

There are a number of important implications arising from this review of overseas experience for the development of effective consumer participation in South Australia. Consumer participation in the electricity industry needs to be well resourced to enable the development of a pool of experienced advocates. These advocates need to be compensated for the many hours they spend doing committee work. They also need the support of suitably trained and qualified professionals. This might be usefully achieved through the development of collaborative research linkages with the university sector. Finally, it is important that consumer organisations maintain a high level of independence from industry and government.

Conclusion

There is a range of pressing consumer and environmental issues facing South Australians as they confront the impact of FRC and the operation of the National Electricity Market. This highlights the need for a well-resourced non-government organisation focussing on small consumer and environmental interests related to the operation of the South Australian electricity market. The early social policy challenges facing such an organisation include the need to advocate to:

- ensure there are enforceable legal obligations on electricity retailers to continue to serve vulnerable consumers such as those on low and fixed incomes
- ensure that there is adequate consumer protection governing the maintenance of advisory services, the use of prepayment meters and time-to-pay provisions
- ensure that electricity retailers are required to:
  - □ develop hardship policies, covering matters such as debt collection and disconnection practices
  - □ make available a variety of easily accessible alternative payment options to make payment of electricity bills easier
- re-assess programs which provide assistance in paying electricity bills such as concessions and energy relief programs
- strengthen public education programs which deal with matters such as prudent energy use
- develop assistance programs to help consumers control their electricity bills by reducing their need for energy.

Environmental policy challenges include the need to set appropriate greenhouse gas reduction targets and the development of a world-leading sustainable energy industry strategy to demonstrate the state government's commitment to combating climate change. Building new industries focussing on the objective of achieving sustainability is another essential element of future policy in this area. Components of such a strategy could include:

- The implementation of demand-side management measures into the market needs to be addressed; for example, before any new augmentation, demand-side management should be considered as the first option.

- Energy-efficiency services need to be offered to consumers by retailers instead of higher consumption being promoted.
- A South Australian renewable energy target additional to the federal 2% renewable target should be established.
- Continuous revisions of the building codes should be undertaken to ensure passive design principles are implemented into all new buildings. Furthermore, building extensions should also be made to meet a required energy efficiency standard.
- Environmental costs, including those associated with climate change, need to be included within the cost–benefit analysis of new investments in the industry.

The consumer and environmental challenges are clear. The shock of a 20–30% increase in the price of residential electricity in 2003 is likely to intensify pressure within the community for consumer interests to be taken more seriously. Waiting until major climate changes occur before environmental concerns are addressed is a short-sighted and risky strategy. Should they rise to the challenge, governments, businesses and communities with the courage to address pressing consumer and environmental concerns will be remembered for leaving the world a better place for today's children.

References

Pareto Associates 2000, 'End-user advocacy in the National Electricity Market', prepared for NECA for consideration in its review of feasibility and resourcing of an NEM End-User Advocacy Group.

Useful websites

www.oecd.org

www.saiir.sa.gov.au

www.ipart.nsw.gov.au

National Consumer Council available at www.ncc.org.uk

Independent gas and electricity consumer council available at www.energywatch.org.uk

National Energy Action available at www.nea.org.uk

CHAPTER 13

The Power to Change

Towards a sustainable and equitable electricity industry

**JOHN SPOEHR, JOHN DENLAY, JOHN LAWRENCE,
DENNIS MATTHEWS AND ANDREW NANCE**

The threat of large electricity price increases early in 2003 requires an urgent policy response from the government. However, the optimum medium-term solution to the electricity price crisis in South Australia involves the development of a strategy for a sustainable energy industry, a strategy which adopts a 'triple bottom line' approach focussing attention on affordability, energy efficiency and the need for renewable energy. The strategy should be designed to integrate the social, economic and environmental objectives crucial to the provision of energy to the community. Moreover, the establishment of an 'authority for environmentally sustainable energy' should underpin this crucial policy area. By integrating the need for affordable energy with energy-demand management and renewable energy initiatives, South Australia could lead the nation in the development of a sustainable energy industry. An industry of the future such as this has the potential to be a major generator of new jobs and exports. The challenge for the government is to provide the leadership necessary to integrate social, economic and environmental objectives into a triple bottom line approach to energy industry policy.

The electricity industry is in need of urgent attention!

The privatisation of the electricity industry in South Australia and South Australia's participation in the National Electricity Market (NEM) have raised concerns in the community about electricity pricing, system reliability and environmental sustainability. It now appears that the government has less capacity to meet social objectives like affordability and reliability, and environmental objectives such as pollution and greenhouse gas emissions. Recent price rises for business consumers heightened fears that supply constraints in South Australia will translate into substantial price increases for domestic consumers. This fear will be realised in 2003.

Privatisation of the electricity industry in South Australia has increased the potential for price shocks. In order to maximise proceeds from the sale of electricity assets, new generation initiatives, with the exception of Pelican Point, were not pursued vigorously by the previous Liberal Government. Since privatisation, the focus of policy has been upon increasing supply through gas- and coal-fired generation capacity and interconnectors. Inadequate attention has been paid to alternative methods of matching supply and demand such as demand-side management measures designed to reduce consumption. The development of renewable sources of energy such as solar and wind power also requires much more attention.

This chapter outlines key electricity policy issues and potential electricity policy reforms in a range of areas including the National Electricity Market, energy and equity, energy efficiency and demand management and renewable energy.

The National Electricity Market

The operation of the NEM currently inhibits the pursuit of broader social, economic and environmental goals. It is difficult to see how these goals will be met without fundamental reform to the operation of the NEM. This could involve:

- restoring the natural monopoly components of the industry – transmission and distribution – to public ownership, with the individual states owning their own networks and the National Grid being jointly owned
- abandoning the idea of competition between distribution networks since a single distribution network for each state would permit investment decisions to be guided by the needs of electricity users rather than by the strategic and regulatory considerations currently dominant

- reforming the pool system which has been abandoned in most other countries and which seems inevitable
- incorporating the real costs of environmental impacts such as air pollution and greenhouse gas emissions into the trading and decision-making of the NEM, perhaps in the form of a carbon tax or the creation of tradable emission permits.

Electricity and equity

In a community experiencing a growing disparity between rich and poor and rising numbers of people in relative poverty, specific policy measures are required to protect the interests of the most vulnerable, and to improve the living standards of and opportunities for low-income households.

Such measures are particularly needed in South Australia now, given that:

- Adelaide electricity prices over the last ten years have shown the second greatest rate of increase among Australian capitals, behind only Hobart.
- Significant tariff increases are widely expected with the introduction of 'full retail contestability' (set for January 2003).
- Low electricity-using households are cross-subsidising high electricity users – especially those using large air-conditioning systems in summer months.

Tariff increases set for all electricity consumers hit low-income consumers harder, representing a higher proportion of household income. Government benefits and concessions have often failed to meet these cost increases over recent years.

Low-income households are unable to lower electricity use easily without a major reduction in their basic living standards. Their housing and appliances are usually older and less efficient. Furthermore, many special uses are health-related and many users are forced, for financial reasons to stay at home during the day, using heating/cooling and other electrical equipment. Energy-efficiency measures typically require upfront costs, which many households simply don't have. And some efficiency measures, such as the government's solar hot water rebate, are not available to rental properties.

Those on low incomes routinely juggle and postpone bill payment. Retailer debt-recovery which is geared to more affluent customers often fails to respond to this situation appropriately. Increasing disconnection and reconnection fees simply deepens the debt problems. Given the importance electricity has in our society, access should be a fundamental right. Disconnection should not be used as a punishment but as a last resort for the small numbers of consumers refusing to pay.

Measures which can address these issues include:

- *Capping prices*: ensuring that low-income electricity consumers experience no surges in electricity tariffs or in related charges (including disconnection fees and other penalties)

- *Concession arrangements*: reviewing these, including the Emergency Electricity Payments Scheme to ensure adequate support for those most in need

- *Consumer retail code*: ensuring that the code and retailers' practice encompass a consumer's 'right to supply', effective debt management strategies, and responsible advertising

- *Communicating*: allaying fears about cost increases under full retail contestability and ensuring the proposed benefits of choice are delivered to all households

- *Electricity debt management*: reviewing education and information strategies

- *Energy-efficiency measures*: consumers exerting more effective control over electricity usage. Measures should include better-targetted education and information on energy efficiency, grants and subsidies for the installation of low-cost energy-efficiency provisions in low-income private and public housing. (This is important as recent bill rises in low-income households appear primarily the result of increased consumption rather than tariff rises).

Electricity efficiency and peak demand management

South Australia is currently in a bind of upwardly spiralling demand for electricity, necessitating very costly supply options to meet this demand. This is largely driven by rapid growth in demand for electricity during hot summer periods. Power stations costing around

$100 million each are being installed to supply power on a handful of days each year. Equally expensive interconnectors are proposed, although there is no guarantee that electricity will flow through them during peak times.

Although the private sector now pays for such investment, SA consumers pay through rising electricity prices. In many cases it is cheaper to conserve electricity than build more power stations or extend networks. Energy efficiency can provide significant financial, social and environmental benefits for a modest amount of government investment. The following section demonstrates how cost-effective residential energy efficiency can be delivered.

Rapid uptake of solar water heaters

Around half of SA households have electric water heaters. It is typically their largest user of electricity and can be responsible for up to 4 tonnes of greenhouse gases each year. With government rebates many solar units pay for themselves in less than their warranty periods. Nevertheless, only around 3% of homes have solar water heating. This situation could be improved by:

- Current solar water rebates could be extended to private rental and housing trust properties. This would allow many low-income households to access solar electricity. Arrangements by which owners lease the units and tenants pay; for example, through electricity bills, will be needed.

- Energy-efficiency requirements for new houses and major renovations could be extended to require energy-efficient water heating, such as that of solar and 5-star gas.

Currently, the potential exists for promoting growth of the local solar energy industry which, in turn, will create local jobs and push down the installation costs of solar water heaters.

Electricity retailer energy-efficiency targets

Experience from NSW shows that home retrofit programs, involving water-efficient shower roses, efficient lighting and draught-proofing can cut over a tonne of greenhouse gas emissions per year and generate cost savings after one to two years. Setting a 10% greenhouse gas reduction target for electricity retailers can foster such programs and establish local businesses in home energy auditing and retrofitting.

Reducing peak demand

Residential peak demand is predominantly caused by growth in air-conditioner use. The peak in demand for electricity is made higher by general appliances used during peak periods. Programs for a reduction in peak demand can be funded by diverting capital from new power stations, network upgrades and interconnectors. Initiatives promoting energy efficiency include:

- retrofitting insulation, shading and draught-proofing in existing housing stock
- education and incentives to retailers of air conditioners to promote efficient models
- education to households on efficient use of air conditioning
- upgrade and retirement programs for old refrigerators, especially second refrigerators.

The implementation of initiatives such as these will require the support of a well-resourced and autonomous authority for environmentally sustainable energy.

Renewable energy

By world standards electricity prices in Australia are extremely low. Furthermore, Australians are, per capita, one of the world's highest users of electricity.

For decades, there have been calls for changes in the way we generate and use energy. Some renewable energy technologies, such as solar hot water generation, are economically competitive in SA. Others, such as photovoltaics (solar cells), are competitive only in certain niche markets. Incentives for reducing greenhouse gas emissions coupled with technological developments mean that wind power is becoming a more cost-effective alternative source of power in SA. Photovoltaic cells for generating electricity from sunlight are similarly becoming more competitive, especially for grid-connected systems. Furthermore, if environmental and social costs (so-called externalities) are calculated into the cost of electricity generation then renewable energy becomes a more competitive prospect.

Renewable energy technologies tend to be smaller, more labour-intensive, less capital-intensive and easier to make locally. This increases local employment, improves balance of trade, and makes financing easier.

In the past the uptake of renewable energy technology in SA has been hampered by non-technical barriers such as subsidies to grid electricity traditionally generated from non-renewable fossil fuels – coal, oil, and gas. Renewable energy suffers a competitive disadvantage because of lack of the infrastructure provided for non-renewable energy. Much public money went into ETSA and the SA Gas Company. There was no equivalent funding for renewable competitors to gas and non-renewable electricity.

Renewable energy is now in a position of having to compete with entrenched mature industries, which are still receiving government subsidies, yet another area which could be addressed by the establishment of an authority for environmentally sustainable energy. The NSW equivalent of such a body, the Sustainable Energy Development Authority (SEDA), has assisted in the development of a more competitive energy market in which renewable electricity products and energy efficiency can compete on equal terms with non-renewable energy.

Power politics and the public interest

Public anxiety about the impact of the privatisation of the electricity industry in South Australia continues to rise in response to power price hikes and events such as the Osborne generation plant crisis caused by the collapse of the US-based energy giant, NRG. While South Australia remains heavily dependent upon transfers of electricity from Victoria, the threat of power shortages at peak times over summer is real. Meanwhile much remains to be done to address pressing environmental imperatives facing the electricity industry. Much faster progress on developing renewable sources of energy and promoting energy efficiency must be made to help reduce greenhouse gas emissions.

The resolution of these problems requires a fundamental re-thinking of the role of government in the electricity industry. Clearly, market-based solutions such as privatisation are not the answer to pressing social, economic and environmental imperatives. If the public interest is to prevail over private interests in shaping the future of the electricity industry, the government will have to intervene on behalf of the wider community. Tom Playford, former Premier of South Australia, recognised this in 1945 when he championed the nationalisation of the privately run industry in South Australia. History has a tendency to repeat itself when the political stakes are high and the costs of doing nothing are great. *Power Politics* poses a challenge to political leaders to repair the damage done by privatisation and chart a new course for a socially and environmentally sustainable electricity industry for the twenty-first century.

THE CONTRIBUTORS

Kathryn Davidson is a project officer with the Centre for Labour Research, University of Adelaide and the Conservation Council of South Australia.

John Denlay works for the South Australian Government on demand-side management issues and strategies. He was formerly the Co-ordinator of the Commonwealth Cool Communities project.

Chris Finn is a lecturer in law at the University of Adelaide

John Lawrence worked as the Low Income Energy Consumers Project Officer with the South Australian Council of Social Service. He is now based at Flinders University.

Dr Dennis Matthews is the energy spokesperson for the Conservation Council of South Australia.

Andrew Nance is an electrical engineer. He is the Co-ordinator of the Commonwealth Government's Cool Communities project in South Australia based at the Conservation Council of South Australia.

Professor John Quiggin is an ARC Senior Fellow based at the University of Queensland.

John Spoehr is the Executive Director of the Centre for Labour Research, University of Adelaide.

EDITOR'S NOTE

Power Politics is the product of eight authors' commitment to raising public awareness about energy issues and challenges. I thank you all for your contributions and dedication throughout the publishing process.

South Australia is fortunate to have a publisher like Wakefield Press. In particular I am very grateful to Michael Bollen and Stephanie Johnston who continue to provide a space for the publication of important South Australian focussed books. The Don Dunstan Foundation and the University of Adelaide have provided financial support for the project.

Special thanks go to Penelope Curtin whose assistance as technical editor ensured that the book is more readable and coherent. Thanks also to Ray Broomhill for providing valuable advice during the editing process.

Finally I wish to thank Jane Rodeghiero for her love and encouragement.

John Spoehr
Adelaide, February 2003

Beyond the Contract State

Ideas for social and economic renewal in
South Australia

Edited by JOHN SPOEHR

Ever wonder why you feel uneasy about the sell-off of South
Australian utilities? Is it true that the state is facing a debt crisis of
overwhelming magnitude? And why do government services seem so
run-down?

With Don Dunstan's 1998 Whitlam Oration as its centrepiece,
Beyond the Contract State offers some of the answers to these and
other perplexing questions. Expert commentators provide fresh
insights and ideas to help stimulate social and economic renewal in
South Australia

For more information visit www.wakefieldpress.com.au

The Wakefield Companion to South Australian History

Editor WILFRED PREST
Managing Editor KERRIE ROUND
Assistant Editor CAROL FORT

The Wakefield Companion to South Australian History is a one-volume guide to events, institutions, people, places, themes and topics of significance in the history of South Australia. It provides an authoritative and comprehensive source of historical background information, presented in readily accessible language and format. While paying attention to distinctive, innovatory and unusual elements in South Australian history, the Companion also underlines the contribution made by South Australians to the broader national culture, polity and society.

The Wakefield Companion to South Australian History is a landmark publication, the first such work of reference for any Australian state or territory. Compiled by an editorial team based in the University of Adelaide, the Companion is a lively, wide-ranging work that incorporates the latest research findings from an outstanding team of 220 expert authors.

For more information visit www.wakefieldpress.com.au

Wakefield Press is an independent publishing and
distribution company based in Adelaide, South Australia.
We love good stories and publish beautiful books.
To see our full range of titles, please visit our website at
www.wakefieldpress.com.au.

Wakefield Press thanks Fox Creek Wines
and Arts South Australia for their support.